The Dog Walker
&
Pet Sitter Bible

The Dog Walker
&
Pet Sitter Bible

Josh Schermer

Published in the United States

ISBN: 978-0-578-03848-3

Typesetting by *www.wordzworth.com*

Set in 11/13 Palatino Linotype

About the Author

Josh Schermer is a lifetime New Yorker and is the owner and founder of Downtown Pets, one of the most respected pet services in New York City. Josh was instrumental in the famous rescue of "Molly the cat" in the West Village of New York City. Josh is a vegan, an environmental entrepreneur and in the past year he made Downtown Pets into a green dog walking company. He is presently starting a new company that will offer cruelty free and animal free products and Josh is donating 10% off all proceeds from this book to The Humane Society of America.

Thanks

I have a lot of people to thank for getting this book finished! I want to thank Marjorie for your amazing edits and overall excitement for the project. I want to thank Chris for the great information you provided. I want to thank Don Kaplan for pushing me to do this project and thank all my friends and family for your belief in me. I want to thank Andrew for being there to talk to and laugh hysterically with. I want to give a special thanks to all of my past and present walkers for the hard work you've put in. But the biggest thanks goes to Sharone, who has been unbelievably helpful in supporting me through this project. I never would have finished this without your help, thanks and love you!

Contents at a Glance

How to Use This Book

Who Is This Book for?

This book is for anyone looking to start his or her own pet service. It doesn't matter if you live in a city or in the country, if you want to start a pet sitting business or become a dog trainer, you will find tons of information in my book.

Search This Book

One of the benefits of an e-book is you can find whatever information you want very quickly. If you're reading this on your computer you'll notice a search bar towards the top right of this page. You can type key words into that search box now or in the future when you come up with questions.

Definitions

The following are definitions for terms you will find used in this book.

Walkers

I will use the word walkers to represent anyone you hire to work for you. It doesn't matter if you create a pet sitting, dog running or dog walking business, etc. When reading this book the word walker will represent the person who works for you.

Employees vs. Independent Contractors

We will discuss the difference between hiring employees vs. independent contractors later in the book. It's up to you what you classify your walkers as but you'll find that I routinely call walkers employees in this book. I do this because I have classified my walkers as employees.

Walking a Route

You will find the term *route* used often in this book. A route can mean the following when it comes to a pet service:

- *A dog walking route*: This usually involves from as little as 7 to as many as 17 dogs being walked on a daily basis.
- *Pet Sitters and Dog Trainers*: Routes usually do not apply to pet sitting or dog trainers. While a pet sitter and dog trainer might get repeat business, often they will be taking care of a new client's pets, so there are no set routes in pet sitting or dog training.
- *A dog running route*: A dog runner usually runs the same dogs on a weekly basis.

A dog running route usually consists of 3-5 runs a day, from 30-45 minutes each.

Sweat equity

Sweat equity involves investing time, money and energy into your business and not being compensated for it now. But sweat equity is meant as an investment in your company that will pay off many times over in the near future.

Individual walk	= Walking a single dog only
Group walk	= Walking 2-4 dogs at one time
Pack walk	= Walking more than 4 dogs at one time

Chapter 1

Getting Started

"A journey of a thousand miles must begin with a single step."

– CHINESE PROVERB

Christmas morning 2002 – my first client

I never set out to create a pet service and certainly not to create one of the largest pet services in New York City, as Downtown Pets has become. Back on Christmas morning 2002 when I visited Downtown Pets' first ever client, I could think no farther than finding a way to pay my bills. I woke up at 6 am on a cold winter morning in New York City and walked over to feed and play with a cat. I was pretty depressed as I walked over to feed that cat, unemployed, lost in life and working on Christmas morning for $10 just seemed to depress me even more. My self-esteem was at an all-time low. I was a person filled with big ideas and passion but had yet to find something in life where I could direct all that energy.

My mood quickly changed though upon opening the door to find a fluffy little cat staring at me down a long hallway. The cat seemed a little apprehensive at the sight of a stranger entering her home but she also seemed happy to have someone visiting her. We quickly became great friends and being able to provide this animal comfort while its owner was away seemed very worthwhile to me. I've always considered myself a protector of animals and the joy I brought this little cat made all my other problems sort of disappear. It seemed like I had finally found something I could believe in: caring for animals. Visiting that cat and working with animals in general was honest, organic work and something I could feel proud of.

"Movies are made before the first day of shooting." - unknown

The beginning of Downtown Pets might have started with those leisurely cat visits on Christmas day but it would soon spiral into a fast-paced, medium-sized business. My rise from a single client to financial freedom might have happened quickly but I paid dearly for not planning ahead. I took on clients anywhere at anytime and it was routine for me to work 100-hour workweeks. Sometimes it got so tough that I would cry at night when I'd get home. There were times where all I did was work and sleep and I didn't actually have time in my day to do anything else. In the end it all worked out but I'd never do it that way again.

Not planning ahead before I started my company wasted my time, wasted my clients and employees time, lost me money, brought me problems I easily could have avoided and in some ways could have led to the downfall of my business. I want to try and help you avoid as much of the stress in starting your company as possible. So to begin let's start creating a framework for your company that can fit your lifestyle both in the present and as your company grows. The aim is for you to create a company that will not only provide you with financial freedom but also personal freedom. I mean, isn't one of the main reasons in owning your own company to have personal freedom? It sure was for me but if you don't plan ahead you might end up with a company you feel a slave to. I want to make sure that you plan ahead so you don't go through the same problems I did.

Experience required

I don't know where in life you are as you read this book, but back before I started my pet service I had no clue what job was right for me. When I looked at want ads in newspapers it was like they were written in Chinese. The skills I had learned so far in life didn't seem to apply to a specific trade and there didn't seem to be a job for me. How many times have we seen the words "experience required" written in a want ad for a job? And it prompts the age-old question: how do you ever get experience if no one will hire you without experience? Well, if there were a want ad describing the pet service you are about to create, you'd also see "experience needed" written. But you know what? No matter who you are, you have the experience needed to create a pet service. In fact you're likely much more prepared to create this pet service than you realize.

Maybe you feel the same way in your life right now that I did when I started Downtown Pets? Maybe you're coming from a job that involved you monotonously doing the same process over and over and over again? Or maybe you're coming from a job where you were an assistant to someone? Or waited on people? Maybe you're coming from a job you felt held you back and didn't allow you to completely realize your true talents? When you work jobs you are not passionate about it can hurt your spirit. But without even realizing it you have been collecting and honing skills from all these jobs, good and bad. For some, like myself, it took creating a business of my own to finally tap into these skills I'd developed.

Past work experiences

I did something very helpful early on in my business. I sat down and created a list of all my past jobs and my past bosses. I wrote down a list of all the positive and negative things I'd learned from these jobs and it turned out to be very educational for me. I was surprised to discover I'd probably learned more *from my bad bosses* than my good ones. I'm sure you've heard people talk about how valuable failures and mistakes are because they allow you to learn from them, to grow and to improve yourself. It might sound cliché until you start running your own business. The good and bad experiences of your past jobs are so real to you and they can positively be applied to your pet service. No matter your work or life experiences, you already have a rich history of experience to pull from.

Creating a company culture from the very beginning

A key factor for both your happiness and the success of your business is to create a company culture as early as possible. What is a company culture? It's the environment you want and/are willing to work within. It's also the environment you want your clients and future employees to work within. (For example: I demand that my walkers and clients return the same respect I give them – they can vent but they can't be disrespectful with me.) This is also your opportunity to make your company represent your values and interests in life (for example: combining my love of the environment with my present business by becoming a green business). And isn't this one of the best parts of creating your own company? Finally getting the chance to create a comfortable environment for you to work within? To finally have true control over what you'll need to endure on a daily basis? Now don't get me wrong, you'll still need to deal with stress and difficult people. But it will be your choice to do so and if you don't want to deal with a person or a situation you can end things on your own terms. This reality of having control over your own environment is a wonderful benefit of owning your own business.

Walk the walk and talk the talk, starting now!

I don't know where you're at as you read this book. Maybe you've never dog walked before and you're getting ready to create your first route? Or maybe you're walking a route already but want to create a few more routes? Or maybe you're already running a pet service but you want to make it better, bigger or tighter? No matter where you are with things I want you to start, from this very moment, speaking from a place of strength when it comes to your pet service.

You can't always control how you feel but you can control what you do

When you're talking to someone about your company I want you to smile, be warm and speak with confidence, even if you don't feel confident. There's a term, "act as if."

Act as if you're really happy even if you're not.

Act as if you operate a big, powerful dog walking company, even if you don't.

Act as if you've been dog walking for 5 years, not 5 weeks.

If you're a small company I want you to act big and strong!

If you're a big company I want you to act small and personal!

What you outwardly portray to potential clients or employees does not have to match how you feel inside. And to be very clear, I am *not* recommending that you lie to people. I am recommending that you feel this confidence, that you believe that it is so. And even if you don't believe it inside, portray it outside and others will think you feel this way. *Act as if.*

Always keep moving

In the following sections you are going to be asked to write down an action plan for the core values of your company. You might think it's a little early in the game to be doing something like that but it's not. It's imperative that from this very moment you start creating a framework for your company. This will help give you direction and confidence. And don't worry about these answers being set in stone either. The mark of a good company is the ability to be flexible and to keep moving. They say if a whale stops moving it can die and that whales even move while they are sleeping. Look at your company in the same light. You must keep moving, keep adjusting to the changing business climate or your company could fail.

Action plan

So let's get started with your action plan and hopefully you can avoid some of the pitfalls I went through. In your action plan you will come up with the following:

- Your company's mission statement.
- Your company's values statement.
- Your company's vision statement.
- Your company's goals.

Mission Statement

To put it simply a *mission statement* establishes what your company is and what it does. You want to make your *mission statement* brief, clear and informative. It should highlight the services you'll offer, where you will offer them and how you'll separate yourself from your competition. Here are some example business mission statements:

Zappos

"...to position Zappos as the online service leader. If we can get customers to associate the Zappos brand with the absolute best service, then we can expand into other product categories beyond shoes."

Sony (1950's)

"Become the company most known for changing the worldwide poor-quality image of Japanese products"

Google Mission

"To organize the world's information and make it universally accessible and useful."

3M

"To solve unsolved problems innovatively."

Here is our mission statement: Downtown Pets

"To offer individual and professional pet services in Lower Manhattan."

Values Statement

A values statement is a set of beliefs and principles that guide the activities and operations of your company. It's important that all your employees are given a copy of your values statement.

What is *your* message? What do *you* believe in? Here is an example of a business's values statement: *Google Values:*

- We want to work with great people.
- Technology innovation is our lifeblood.
- Working at Google is fun.
- Be actively involved; you are Google.
- Don't take success for granted.
- Do the right thing; don't be evil.
- Earn customer and user loyalty and respect every day.
- Sustainable long-term growth and profitability are key to our success.
- Google cares about and supports the communities where we work and live.
- We aspire to improve and change the world.

Here are our values: Downtown Pets' Values

- Offer individual dog walkers and a personal approach.
- Your dog's safety & happiness comes before anything.
- Have a positive & lasting impact on your dog's life.
- Teach new dog walkers the basics of dog training.
- Provide excellent customer service for both our clients and their dogs.

Vision Statement

A vision statement paints a picture of what your company wants to become. To those inside and outside of your company your vision is your compass showing the world the direction in which your company is headed. It not only points you to the future, it makes you want to jump up and get headed there.

Apple

"To change the world through technology."

Downtown Pets

"We want to be *the best* dog walking company in New York City, not *the biggest*."

Set some goals for your company and yourself

It's important that you routinely set some goals for your company to reach. I actually create new goals for my company to reach every quarter of the year. It's helpful for me and my walkers to have something to work towards. I call this my quarterly action plan. It's also important for your goals to be measurable and/or to be met within a time frame.

Here is an example of some goals you might set in the beginning of your company:

- I want to have at least 5 clients within the next 3 months.
- I want to hire my first (or my next) employee within the next 9 months.
- I want to become an expert on all issues related to puppies.
- I want to put 10% of my weekly profits into a savings account.

Your goals might be different than what I wrote here but what's important is that you give yourself something to work towards.

End of chapter checklist

- Make a list of your past work experiences. Have it include the good and bad of what you experienced and learned.
- Come up with a mission statement for your company.
- Come up with a values statement for your company.
- Come up with a vision statement for your company.
- Come up with goals for your company to achieve.

Chapter 2

What Type of Pet Service is Right For You?

What type of pet service do you want to create?

It seems like a simple question but there are many different types of pet services out there. And each type of pet service poses it's own unique risks, rewards and responsibilities. Now is the time when you'll want to consider what type of pet service is right for you. When thinking about what type of service is right for you consider some of the following:

- How big do you want your pet service to become?
- How much responsibility do you want to have?
- How many hours a week do you want to work?
- How early do you want to start working?
- How late do you want to stop working?
- Until what hour can clients call you?

- Do you want to offer a very personal service with a high price point (like Starbucks)? Or a less personal service with very low prices (like Walmart)?

- What areas/neighborhoods would you like to offer service?

- Do you want to have to manage employees working for you or do you want to work alone?

- Do you want to offer service on nights and weekends? What if you or your walker can't cover the walk? Who will back it up? You?

- What type of lifestyle do you want to live?

The answers to the above questions might not be so clear to you presently but it's important to give yourself some type of parameters to work within. You can also update these answers over time as your company evolves.

Example: As a company we didn't offer consistent weekend dog walking because there wasn't a demand for it. When a client would request a dog walk on the weekend we'd cover it if we were able to but it wasn't a guarantee. Now we have started to offer consistent Saturday dog walks and we're trying to create a market for this service. What changed? We took our time to create a system that would allow us to offer the same quality in our weekend walks that we offer in our weekly walks. My belief is if you're going to offer a service you need to offer it with the same conviction you do everything else.

Special Note: You will find the term dog walker used often in this book and the majority of the book will be dedicated to dog walking and pet sitting. But the information, methods and philosophies discussed in this book can be applied to any type of pet service you want to create.

Types of services

Read all the pet service descriptions below very closely. You never know. You might want to add on additional services now or in the future.

You hear the term "pet services" thrown around so much but what does it actually mean? Well there's the obvious part that it includes pets but the directions you can take working with pets are plentiful. In the following lists I've tried to paint as vivid a picture as possible on what each pet service would be like for you. Of course you'll need to experience them for yourself but this should get you thinking what service might be best for you.

1. A dog walking and pet sitting company

Description: A dog walking and pet sitting business involves walking dogs on a daily basis. A walker will walk anywhere from 5-20 dogs in a day. Some companies offer individual dog walking only while others offer group walks, but usually not more than 4 dogs at a time. A dog walking business involves a lot of daily customer service, feedback and organization. You need to have backup plans in place for when walkers get sick, injured and/or leave early. You'll need to fully train your walkers and have mechanisms to monitor them. Clients who use a daily dog walker usually work regular 9am-5pm business days, Monday- Friday. The majority of your dog walking clients need you to get their dog outside to go to the bathroom, get some exercise, some socialization with other dogs and some love while they are gone. There will also be clients who are home but like the consistency of the schedule a dog walker will keep with their dog. A dog walker allows them to do what they want to do and not have to worry about walking their dog at a specific time. The more knowledge you have of dogs the more services you can offer to your clients (puppy services, house training, leash training, obedience training, basic commands, etc.). Clients looking for a company expect to have a dedicated backup walker when their regular walker gets sick, goes on vacation or moves on. Company clients expect a level of professionalism like being able to pay with a credit card and submitting schedule changes online.

Note: Daily dog walking might be more of a city thing but you can create a demand for this service anywhere. Daily dog walks help with the health, happiness of the dog, house training, keeping a schedule, etc. This is where your knowledge of dogs will really benefit you.

What it requires from you: A dog walking business is a very personal relationship and it will require lots of contact through email and over the phone. Professional dog walkers should be more educated on dogs than their clients are (you need to be able to help and point out issues to the client; if not you can be replaced by a 6th grader. Not everyone will require or expect you to be so knowledgeable, but it's rare a client will not respect or appreciate that fact).

Hours: 9am-5pm Monday-Friday for dog walking; seven days a week and 24 hours a day for pet sitting.

Example Services: Dog walks can range from 15 minutes to 30 or 60 minutes at a time. Most dogs will go outside once a day but younger dogs could use 2-3 visits a day.

Startup Time: An individual route should not take more than 3-5 months for you to create. From there your next few routes should take 2-4 months each and after a year to a year and a half they should take 1-3 months depending on your attention to marketing.

Startup Costs: Minimal but lots of sweat equity.

Commitment: You could maintain a 2nd part-time job in the beginning of building an individual route. But as you get people working for you and make it a real company it will become very difficult to maintain a second job.

Dangers: You start to offer anything, anywhere, at any time, and start working 7 days a week, 12-15 hours a day. You create no boundaries for your clients and you become miserable. It can become difficult to cover routes when walkers are sick, get fired, quit, etc. You need to be able to keep up with hiring and training great walkers to meet your growth.

2. A purely pet sitting business and in-home boarding

Description: This service requires staying in an owner's home or taking a client's dog into your own home when they are away. Similar to the dog walking, pet sitting means a lot of feedback to owners on how things are going. No matter which pet service you decide to create, you'll need to have your clients fill out an application before beginning service but nowhere is the clients' personal information more important than when it comes to pet sitting. With a client gone and maybe unreachable you need to make sure you have all the extra numbers like emergency contacts, vet contact, an after hours/24hr vet if their normal vet doesn't offer 24hr service, building super, management numbers and always make sure you have a credit card on you for emergencies. You will also need to make sure you know about the dog's general temperament: Aggressive? In heat? Etc. You will need to decide if you are going to do a sleepover while walking dogs on the weekend too. This is a numbers game. You get a lot of pet sitters so you can cover a ton of dogs – having independent contractors is the best structure for this company. This type of business is a little less stressful in that your pet sitters are not maintaining a full route of dogs to walk everyday. This business involves your pet sitters staying at the home of a dog owner who is away on vacation, etc. or the pet sitter might take the dog into their own home. If you find trustworthy pet sitters this can be a pretty low maintenance operation compared to a daily dog walking company. My concern about someone just being a pet sitter for you and not a dog walker is that you will not often see them perform the job. Make sure to check in on your pet sitters periodically, have checks and balances, etc. to make sure they are doing a good job. With a pet sitting/boarding company you need to be available all days of the week and at all hours in case something goes wrong – though this should be rare. You also need backup coverage for if someone falls through.

What it requires from you: The nice part about pet sitting, is that you do not have that Monday through Friday, nine to five rush that you get from a dog-walking company. Your sitters are dealing with one dog as opposed to between 9 and 15, so it's not as nerve-racking to help out during the day if they need it. Some of your sitters will stay at the owners' apartments and others will take the pets into their own homes. In this environment, pets will receive more attention than usual and because of this, dogs will usually require less walks. Everyone needs this service at one time or another and you can get tons of referrals from dog- walking businesses that either do not offer pet-sitting or cannot handle their workload. To run a successful pet-sitting business you will need to have access to reliable, trust-worthy sitters and offer your services 24/7. Also, you will need to be able to receive calls and respond at any time to ensure you are not only a director of others but also their manager.

Hours: 24/7. However, your actual time on task will be minimal. It requires just enough time to schedule visits, and be in contact with sitters and clients.

Example services: A pet sit can take place in a client's home or in the home of your pet sitter. Pet sits can last from as short as one night to over a month!

Startup Time: Within 4-6 months you should have a steady part-time income yourself and be in a position to start hiring pet sitters to work for you.

Startup Costs: Minimal but lots of sweat equity to get your name out there.

Commitment: Part-time at first but if you get to the point of having a few people working for you, you'll need to be available at random hours of the day, any day of the week. You need to make sure you always have backup plans in place to cover a job if one of your sitters gets sick, has a problem, etc.

Dangers: You do not adequately screen and/or monitor your pet sitters. An animal gets injured or off leash because of poor supervision and training. The owners are gone, so there are usually not a lot of back-up plans. If your walker calls you up at 11:30 pm and says he's sick and needs to go home, you or someone else needs to get over there. It's not really open to question—someone has to be there. Will it be you? Or will you have an emergency sitter already prepared and even paid a small amount to always be ready to go somewhere on short notice? You will also need to provide the sitter with all of the owners and pet's vital contact and health information (you will need this information on hand too).

3. A dog running business

Description: This service responds to the need (especially in crowded, small living-space types of cities) for dogs to have open space to run and get exercise. People who request this service have probably noticed that their dogs are stressed out, anxious, over-weight, hyper-energetic or have separation anxiety. This is a unique and relatively new type of service that has a high price point. Depending on where in the country you are starting this type of service, you may be impacted greatly by the weather and need to consider very specifically what types of people will be willing to do this hard work. Because this is a new idea to many people, you have the opportunity to corner the market in your area, which may require a great deal of marketing and PR. Because of the business's high price point, you will need fewer clients to make good money. This means lower maintenance for covering routes however it will take longer to create a full company.

What it requires from you: Again, this is a new concept in pet services. What this means for you is that you may need to spend a bit more time to convince potential clients why they need this service. You need to be committed to marketing and come up with ways to do PR. Creative marketing will be key to making your business grow.

Hours: Mornings and end of days Monday through Friday.

Example services: The typical run time for a dog is 45 minutes but smaller dogs should go for 20 or 30 minute runs.

Startup Time: It should take roughly 2-4 months for you to create a part-time route. It should take roughly 2-3 months for you to create each additional route because this is a specialized service.

Startup Costs: Minimal but sweat equity.

Commitment: Small, but you must carefully screen your runners and keep track of the dogs' health.

Dangers: You get injured or your runners get injured. You don't have back up runners. You run dogs that are too young or you run dogs too quickly and they get injured. You don't clearly communicate the need for your service and therefore impede your company's growth.

4. A walk and train service

Description: A walk and train business offers everything a dog walking company does but you can also train the dogs while walking with them. You hire walkers with a strong interest in dog training and dog psychology. In this type of service it is necessary to spend more focus and expectation on the walkers' part concerning the issues a dog may have. Because this service offers more focus on each dog's specific training needs, it has a higher price point than traditional dog walking. Your company will be making a significant impact on the lives of the dogs and the clients. Most likely, a service like this would also offer pet sitting but again, at a higher price point because of the focus on training.

What it requires from you: Offering training services in addition to walking means that you will need to educate yourself as well as your walkers on many different aspects of dogs. You will need to be prepared to field questions in many different categories and must be willing to have discussions with clients and provide them with explanations of what you are doing and why. You will also need to have a way to screen the people you hire with an eye on their attention to detail.

Example services: Walk and train companies offer the same services as a dog walking and/or pet sitting company but they also offer the added feature of reinforcing basic training.

Hours: 9am-5pm Monday through Friday

Startup Time: It should take no more than 4-6 months to create an individual route. Because this is a specialized and expensive service, you will grow slower than a dog walking company or will need to offer both types of services.

Startup Costs: Minimal but will take more sweat equity and time spent learning than a dog walking company.

Commitment: This business takes a larger commitment than a dog walking company. You are not only walking the dogs, you are training them too. You must find and train walkers interested in dog psychology to work for you.

Dangers: You are not able to find walkers who can support your training methods and clients feel your service is weak. Your training methods are not realistic, they are too complicated for your clients to grasp and apply themselves. You do not train the clients and therefore, there will not be many changes for their dogs.

5. *A dog trainer*

Description: To become a legitimate dog trainer you need to become a certified dog trainer. You help clients with all the issues their dogs might be having (house training, leash training, puppy training, basic obedience, basic commands, aggression, separation anxiety, barking, etc.). Part of your interaction will be with the dogs and owners together so you will need to be able to teach both at the same time! As a dog trainer you might find it more difficult to teach the owners than the dogs! It's customary to have a consultation meeting with the dog owners to meet their dogs in their own environment and discuss/view the issues they are having. As an individual dog trainer you might want to consider hiring a few employees to walk dogs for you too. This way you can cover more ground at once, have your walkers reinforcing what you've taught the dogs and the owners and create an additional revenue stream.

What it requires from you: A space to work with dogs both inside and out. Preferably, the space will simulate a home environment. A deep understanding of dog development and a solution oriented attitude.

Hours: Sporadic hours spread out through all days of the week (less hours a day but maybe more days).

Startup Time: Within 6 months, this could become a steady 2nd income, but it might take between a year and a year and a half before it becomes a full-time profession.

Startup Costs: On the high end for this industry. You'll need to get certified which will cost a few thousand dollars, and then you'll need to do all the marketing work that the other businesses require. Estimated startup costs are $3,000 to $7,000.

Commitment: A strong commitment to dog training and dog psychology. You will need to get certified and get your name out there.

Dangers: You spend all the money and time to get certified only to learn that while you love dogs, you don't necessarily love dog training. You learn how to train dogs, but not the dogs' owners (which is *most* important). You like animals but not people and it shows. You can't hustle. *You will need to hustle a lot to make this a full-time profession.*

6. Pooper scooper pickup

Description: A pooper-scooper client lets their dog run freely in a yard and go to the bathroom in the yard. So this service would *not* have a high demand in city areas. A pooper-scooper client either doesn't have the time or interest in cleaning up all this dog waste and that's where you come in. This type of business possesses low start up costs, has a high profit potential and you can even operate this type of business on a part-time basis.

What it requires from you: Dog waste smells obviously, can attract flies and can even be a health hazard if left for too long. Dog waste can seep into water systems if left unattended. This job involves scooping dog waste off clients' yards and disposing of it. Dogs often choose specific areas of the yard to go and you'll find lots of dog waste concentrated in certain areas of the yards. It's physically hard work both in the actual work performed and in dealing with the inclement weather. Dog waste can be heavy depending on the amount you're picking up but also the time of year. During the winter dog waste will be harder and weigh more. During the summer the dog waste will weigh less but you also might get less work with more people home during that time. And the actual process of leaning down and scooping up the dog waste can put strain on your back and your knees so you should try and stretch before, during and after your days work. Removing the dog waste can be an issue, especially depending on where you live. In some areas you're not allowed to mix dog waste with household waste. You should check and see what the dog-waste disposal policy is where you live. In some areas you can rent a bin for when you start to get a lot of clients while in others you can freely dispose of it in garbage cans. But please verify the answer to this question before proceeding both for the environment and the success of your business.

Hours: Hours of operation are not set in stone but 9am-5pm can be assumed.

Startup Time: You should be able to start-up a steady part-time job within 2-3 months.

Startup Costs: Your startup costs are minimal and include some basic marketing, sweat equity on street PR work and some equipment (like rakes, garbage pans, etc). You will need a car to carry all these items from customer to customer and you'll need to be able to carry and dispose of all the waste.

Commitment: While there might be less organization involved with a pooper- scooper business than some other pet services, the experience you have with your employees might be trickier. One of the major things you usually have going for you when hiring someone to work with pets is the ability to work with pets one on one. But in a pooper-scooper business you are basically offering a physical labor job. Your employees might never even interact with the dog whose waste they are disposing of so keep that in mind when listening to the expectations and interests of your applicants.

Dangers: You don't hire competent people and you don't dispose of waste properly. You don't hire enough people and can't handle the workload. You take on too much of the workload yourself, don't arrange for backup help and physically hurt yourself so you can't cover the work anymore.

Additional pet service types

- *Dog Grooming (in-house/your own store/mobile truck):* All dogs need to be groomed, bathed and have their nails clipped. So it's not a surprise that the dog grooming business is on fire. Becoming a dog groomer will involve going to a dog grooming school. I would recommend working in a store or for another dog groomer before going on your own. This job involves patience and a willingness to get bitten as well as scratched.

The profit potential for a dog groomer is high, especially if they can get a few other people working for them too.

- *Dog photographer:* Dog photographers are becoming more prevalent as people want a loving memory of their dogs or just love the idea of their dog being in a photo shoot. There is no required training for this business except having people enjoy your photography. You can either take photos inside a client's home, outside on a walk, or in your own studio. Depending on the type of photos you want to specialize in you might have to go with the studio option and that will require more money (lighting, equipment, etc.). You will need to be good with animals and have the ability to get them to sit still. Most good dog photographers have someone who helps them with the pets while they take pictures (they are called wranglers). The price point for this business is high but your chance of repeat business from the same clients is small.

Note: You'll *not* find daycare or boarding in a facility listed or discussed in this book. I am not a proponent of this type of pet care. I'm sure there are many wonderful boarding facilities but I don't think anything can be more positive for a dog than an in-home experience.

The following details some of the lifestyle requirements for each major pet service I have just described.

Requires you to be available Monday-Friday
Dog walking, dog running, walk and train

Is a seven day a week 24 hour a day commitment
Pet sitting

Involves more of a sporadic schedule
Dog trainer, pooper scooper

Involves low startup costs
Dog walking, pet sitting, dog running, pooper scooper, walk and train

Involves higher startup costs
Dog trainer

Can quickly grow into a company
Pet sitting

Can quickly grow into an individual route
Dog walking, dog running, walk and train, pooper scooper

Requires employees to be a company/career
Pet sitting, dog running, pooper scooper

Does not require employees to be a company/career
Dog walking, walk and train, dog trainer

Requires a high level of dog knowledge
Walk and train, dog trainer

Requires less dog knowledge (not that you should know less but you can)
Dog walking, pet sitting, dog running, pooper scooper

Requires a part-time secretary once it becomes a company
Dog walking, walk and train

Lots of competition in the market
Dog walking, pet sitting

Less competition in the market
Dog running, walk and train, dog trainer, pooper scooper

Less ability to monitor your employees
Pet sitting

More ability to monitor your employees
Dog walking, dog running, walk and train, pooper scooper

Most profit potential
Dog walking, pet sitting, walk and train, dog trainer

Highest price point per job
Dog running, dog trainer

Best potential to make the most money over time
Dog walking, pet sitting, dog trainer

Most responsibility
Dog walking, pet sitting, dog trainer, walk and train

Chapter Checklist

- Look over the different pet service types and decide which one(s) are right for you.
- Remember that you can add on additional service in the future when you're ready.

Chapter 3

Working with Dogs Outside of the Home

"If you want to write for the New York Times, start by sweeping their floors."

- Don Kaplan (Friend/Mentor)

Make yourself indispensable to your clients

If you're just taking a dog to go out to the bathroom and not much else you are easily replaceable and in this competitive marketplace you need to make yourself indispensable. Part of how you do this is to start learning today as much you can about pet health, care and psychology *and never stop learning*. If you're a dog walker and don't know the signs of a sick/hurt dog, know how to stop a dog from pulling or how to house train, etc. then what's the difference between you and the 5th grader across the street?

And oh yeah, your knowledge of dog issues could contribute an additional 20-30% in business! My knowledge of house training alone has contributed that much more business to Downtown Pets.

Some of our keys to dog walking are

Some key factors when you're outside with the dogs:

- Make sure your dogs can at the very least sit (put their butt down), stay (stay in sit), heel (do not pull past you) and come (have the dog come to you when you call it) *on command*. You can view videos tutorials on how to perform a sit, stay, etc. on our website.

- Always walk the dogs on the left side of your body (this establishes consistency for the dogs and is the first step in training a dog) when walking a dog individually.

- Always walk dogs short on the leash (for safety and training).

- Never let go of a leash while on a walk (for safety).

- Look ahead as you walk a dog (avoid problems ahead of time).

- Put knots in your leash about a foot and a half up from the clip and then another about another foot and a half from that first knot. This helps get a dog used to the area they can walk within, helps you teach a dog to heel and it also helps you grip the leash.

- Use 6 foot nylon leashes (anything longer hurts your ability to train the dog and in some areas of the country anything longer is actually illegal).

- Do *not* use retractable leashes (they can be unreliable, unsafe and unprofessional looking).

- Try to always carry treats while on your walks for positive reinforcement Use treats sparingly to reward/reinforce positive behavior in your dogs. Don't use treats often or you'll become a hostage to them and the dogs will think every time they stop they are going to be rewarded. Treats are also a great way to motivate dogs in general and especially dogs that are not yet good walkers.

- Only use the owner's treats or treats approved by the owner (some dogs have allergies to certain ingredients).

- If a dog picks something up with their mouths immediately put your hand to the back of his tongue and scoop out whatever he picked up (don't waste a split second – do you want to have to worry about what the dog just swallowed?).

Special note: You can learn more about many of the things you'll read in this chapter on our website, through videos, images and discussions.

The traits of a good dog walker

- *Engaged with their dogs*: A good dog walker makes eye contact with their dogs and speaks to their dogs periodically through the walk. They speak to a dog in a high pitch voice. Dogs find a high-pitched voice to be welcoming.

- *Avoids danger ahead of time*: A good dog walker doesn't continue to walk into danger areas over and over again without noticing. They direct most of their attention to what is in front of the dogs. A good dog walker sees a problem way ahead of time and avoids it with plenty of space to spare.

- *Carries backup equipment*: You never know if you'll need a backup leash, collar, etc. and you should carry extra equipment with you at all times.

- *Walks dogs on the left side of their body*: Nothing looks more professional than a dog walking short and on the left side of your body.

- *Not on their cell phone through the walks*: Have you ever seen someone walking a dog while talking on their cell phones? If so they were probably not engaged with the dogs they were walking. A dog walker can not give a dog their full attention while yapping on the phone all day.

- *Not dragging or yanking dogs*: You should never drag a dog down the street. It looks terrible, it's mean and there are many other solutions to get a dog to walk.

- *Wears a cell phone earpiece*: Of course you'll need to take some phone calls during your walks but they should be short, you should stop walking the dog while you speak and/or you should use a wired earpiece. Using a wired earpiece allows you to still use both of your hands while you walk the dogs and on a side note I don't think wireless/Bluetooth earpieces are safe to use (based on the radiation they emit).

- *Notices the problems their dogs are having*: A good dog walker should notice if a dog is limping, has a loose stool, throws up and/or has low energy, among other things.

- *Carries waste bags*: It might sound silly but it looks pretty unprofessional to see someone searching for a way to pickup a dog's stool. It looks even more unprofessional to see a dog walker not pickup a dog's stool *at all* (and in some areas it's against the law not to pickup after a dog).

- *Can use and recommend the most proper equipment*: A good dog walker should know how to use all the main equipments made for dogs. They should also be able to recommend equipment to a client if they think it will improve the experience of walking the dog.

- *Educated on the basics of house training, leash training and puppy training*: A good dog walker ideally knows more about dog training and psychology than their clients do.

- *Doesn't force their views on their clients*: Some clients will want you to decide everything for them while others will not want any advice on how to care for their dogs. Make sure that you don't become too pushy with clients when it comes to advice on their pets.

- *Leaves polite and upbeat messages for their clients*: A good dog walker should be polite and upbeat in their messages even on day they are not in a good mood. Be extra careful not to write your messages in a way that could be misunderstood. What client wants to come home to read a message that sounds passive, aggressive, blunt or bossy? Speak clearly, positively, with optimism and use lots of smiley faces and in your messages!

- *Doesn't walk more then 3-4 dogs at a time*: Personally I prefer individual dog walks, or 2 dogs walked at a time only but I do feel you can have a positive walk with 3-4 dogs at a time. Walking anything more than 3-4 dogs at a time looks unprofessional and can be chaotic and dangerous.

- *Sit stays*: At certain times you will need to be able to control the dog you are walking. A good dog walker can put a dog in a sit stay at will because they have practiced putting the dogs into a sit stay (explained later).

- *Give their dogs lots of love*: I'm amazed how I see some dog walkers never give love to the dogs they walk. Make a point of rubbing your dog's chests periodically through your walks.

The traits of an unprofessional dog walker

An unprofessional dog walker does the following:

- *Walks more than 4 dogs at a time (is a pack walker):* As I already mentioned walking more than 4 dogs at a time can be chaotic and dangerous. How can you possibly be aware of the safety and wellbeing of more than 4 dogs at one time out on a walk? You simply can't. Does that mean all pack walkers are unprofessional walkers? No, there are some amazing pack walkers who love dogs, do an outstanding job with their dogs and I would like personally. I just happen to disagree with them on what's best for a dog's safety, training and happiness. Think about it: What do you do with a dog on a pack walk when they don't want to walk? What about a dog who has diarrhea and continues to stop to go the bathroom when a pack walker is in a hurry? Or what if a dog has hurt its paw and started to limp? The dog who doesn't want to walk might get dragged, the dog with diarrhea will get dragged too while they are trying to go to the bathroom and the dog with the hurt paw? It might not even get noticed by the pack walker. Again, this is not a personal attack against pack walkers. I just don't agree with this method of dog walking as a positive option for the dog or the walker.

- *Listens to music while walking a dog:* How can you be aware of your surroundings if you can't hear your surroundings?

- *Smokes cigarettes while walking dogs:* A dog walker smoking a cigarette looks unprofessional but it's also dangerous. A cigarette is a burning ember and if a dog ever leaped up towards your hands, or if you needed to use both of your hands you could have a big problem.

- *Drinks a warm beverage while walking a dog:* This poses the same issues as smoking a cigarette. A warm beverage could spill on a dog or burn them and you don't have use of both hands while carrying the warm beverage.

- *Actively talks on the phone while walking dogs:* There have been studies that have proven that if someone talks on the phone while driving a car it's as dangerous as if they were drunk! Well a dog walker talking on their phone all through their walks is just as dangerous as if they were drunk! If you are concentrated on your phone conversation you can't give the dogs your full attention. And if you're not using an earpiece and instead are holding the phone to your head you don't have use of both of your hands.

- *Is not engaged with their dogs:* It's depressing to me to see a dog walker who just doesn't seem to even notice the dog they are walking. If it looks depressing to me it will also look depressing to clients.

- *Doesn't carry waste bags:* Imagine a dog walker who scurries around trying to find a plastic bag in a garbage can? Or picks up some leaves to try and pick up a dog's stool? It would look pretty silly right? And not just look silly it would be really *annoying and nasty* for the walker.

- *Not aware of their dog's issues:* You're not in tune with your dogs if you don't notice a limp in their walk, blood in their stool, low energy, etc. On top of being able to help your dogs with their issues you will earn appreciation from your clients.

- *Doesn't check the fit of equipment:* A unprofessional dog walker does not check the fit of the dog's equipment *every single time they put the equipment on!* More important than knowing how to put on equipment is making sure it can't come off.

- *Doesn't know equipment:* A poor dog walker uses equipment they aren't familiar with. They don't educate themselves on all the major equipments used by dog owners and can't recommend better equipment than their clients are presently using.

- *Is pushy:* A poor dog walker tries to force their ideas onto a client whether the client is receptive to those ideas or not.

- *Is rude:* You're working in someone else's home, with their dog. You can't be rude to this person. If they even perceive you to be rude or passive- aggressive do you think they'll want you back into their home?

- *Explores the client's home:* A dog walker should pick up their dogs and go straight outside. You should not venture into areas of the house that do not apply to performing your job. A client will likely fire you if you venture into closed bedrooms, closets, use their computer/telephone without permission, etc.

Positive reinforcement

I strongly believe in positive reinforcement when it comes to working with dogs. Positive reinforcement, as you would guess, involves praising dogs for doing something you've asked them to do. It does *not involve yelling at dogs, being forceful with dogs, embarrassing dogs and/or hurting dogs.* I wouldn't recommend aggressive approaches with your own dogs let alone someone else's dogs.

Example of positive reinforcement

You ask a dog to sit and after a few moments they put their butt down on the ground and you praise them by saying, "good dog," and you give them a treat.

Example of aggressive training

You ask a dog to sit and after a few moments of it not responding you force their butt onto the ground by pushing down on their back. Once their butt reaches the ground you don't praise them. And as they say, "a dog remembers what you praise them for much more than what you scold them for."

Corrections

It's important to let a dog know when you're not happy with what they are doing (pulling past you, jumping up on you, leaping at other dogs, etc.). Two important things with correcting dogs are:

- *Be consistent*: If you give a dog mixed messages you will confuse them. If you sometimes allow a dog to do one thing but don't other times you are not being fair to the dog. It's important that you are consistent with both what you say to correct dogs and when you say it. If you're trying to stop a dog from pulling past you, you might say "heel" each time it happens. Or you might use the "ahh ahh ahh" sound we discussed and check the dog when it tries to pull past you.

The point is to use the same term/sound every time you correct a dog and to be consistent in always correcting the habit you're trying to change.

- *Praise at the right times*: One of the biggest sins committed by dog owners is reinforcing negative behaviors. It's very important that you and the owners understand when to praise a dog. In short you want to praise a dog once it has followed your correction.

Example: You are walking a dog that gets very anxious around other dogs. You see a dog coming towards you and immediately see your dog start getting anxious. This would be the very worst moment to praise/treat your dog. Why? Because what you're doing is actually supporting the anxiety the dog is having. What should you do? You want to either put your anxious dog into a sit stay until the other dog walks by you or turn directions and walk away from the 2nd dog. Once the 2nd dog has walked by you or once you have walked away from the 2nd dog you'll want to praise the dog. The dog will remember that when they *didn't get anxious they were praised.*

You and the clients need to speak the same language

It's important that you and the clients speak the same language to their dogs. If a client uses a different command than you do to get a dog to stop pulling you should adopt the client's term. When both the client and walker speak the same language the dogs you will see much better results and much happier dogs.

Being the pack leader

It's very important that you establish yourself as the pack leader with all your dogs from the very beginning. Being the pack leader does not involve using force or even speaking strongly to the dogs you walk. It just involves you establishing a leadership position with the dogs you walk. Part of doing so involves walking ahead of the dogs you walk.

Going through doors, building corners and traffic areas *ahead* of the dogs

One of the easiest ways to establish your role as pack leader is to *not* let the dogs pull ahead of you. You should walk through doors, into elevators, out of buildings, through crosswalks, etc. ahead of the dogs you are walking. At the very least the dogs you are walking should not be walking ahead of you. On top of this establishing your role as pack leader it is also the safest way to walk a dog.

Stopping a dog from pulling ahead of you

Teaching a dog to heel

Teaching a dog to heel is one of the best presents you can give yourself and your clients. Imagine they hire you just to take their dog out to go to the bathroom and maybe a short walk and what do they also get? A dog that now walks better and follows basic commands. By doing these things you're starting to make yourself a professional dog walker and separating yourself from the competition.

Keep in mind when working with a dog on the leash that they very likely *are not* kept in a heel by their owners. Some owners will actually walk their dogs off leash so walking properly on the leash with you might be a brand new experience for some dogs. At Downtown Pets we use three main ideas to help dogs not pull:

- Checking.
- Using your voice/sound (ahh, ahh, ahh).
- The correct equipment.

Checking

Have you ever watched the Dog Whisperer on TV? Do you notice how he checks the dogs by snapping back on the leash? What he's doing is getting the dogs attention and bringing the dog back into his world.

Now we don't recommend you snap back on the leash like he does because he is a uniquely gifted dog trainer whose understanding of dogs is hard to match. But we also don't recommend snapping back on the leash because it's not a form of training we support and it's also not conducive for your dogs and their owners. You can achieve the idea of checking the dog without using a choker or prong collar and without snapping back on the leash with force. In fact with many dogs you might just be able to shake the leash to get the dog's attention. In the worst case, you can do what we call a shake-pull of the leash.

Using your voice to keep a dog in heel

Dogs are very responsive to sound. I was working with a trainer one day who was using a prong collar on a dog (not a piece of equipment I like) and each time the dog would try and pull ahead she would snap the leash back. And each time she snapped the leash back you'd hear the crunching sound of the metal in the prong collar. Then the dog trainer took off the prong collar and attached the leash to a nylon collar. She pulled out a set of keys and the next time the dog tried to pull she shook her keys and the dog pulled back into heel. What's my point? Dogs can be as attentive if not more attentive to your voice, commands, tone, etc. as they can to any other method of training.

When the dog starts to pull past you confidently utter the sound "ah ah ah" and shake the leash back against the dog. If the dog ignores you and continues to pull then stop dead in your tracks. After a few moments the dog should look back. At this moment you can either point to your heel and reward the dog for coming back to heel or you can praise the dog for turning back and continue on your walk. Be consistent with this method and you should see signs of improvement, sometimes even immediately. But remember that each dog is different and each dog like each human has its own learning style and pace. One dog might get it on the 4th to 5th try while another might take weeks. Enjoy the small victories of the slow learner as much as, if not more than the quick learners. Don't have the same expectations of the slow learner as you do of the quick learner or you will frustrate the slow-learning dog and probably have a bad walk that day. The dogs will grow to learn that if they pull ahead they get checks and/or their walk stops. Dogs want to keep the party moving and should grow to walk in step with you.

What are some other techniques for dogs pulling on the leash?

- Change directions: continue to change the direction you're walking until the dog stops pulling/relaxes.
- Put the dogs in sit stays.
- Continuing to put a dog in sit stays when it pulls gets boring for the dogs.

Dogs who are being tough on the leash

Even the best walking dogs can have bad days on the leash. Maybe it's one of those spring days where the dog you're walking can't stop marking everything they see. Or maybe you have a dog who has most definitely emptied themselves, gone #1 a few times, gone #2 a few times but is a bit obsessive and won't stop trying to go.

First off try turning the dog around and walking it in the opposite direction. If it tries to start going again turn around again. The idea you should be conveying to the dog is, "if you don't relax, if you don't come back into my world we're going to keep going in circles."

You can view videos that will visually display many of the training philosophies discussed in this book here: Log onto *www.petsitterbible.com* > click on the "videos" tab

Those dogs who keep putting their butts down on the ground

I have found this is a much tougher dog to work with than the dog that pulls. There is an entire industry dedicated to making products to stop dogs from pulling but I can't think of one product to help you keep a dog moving forward. So over time I've had to develop my own methods and here are some.

- Plain and simple just try and keep moving forward. Outside of normal bathroom break stops or a dog that is exhausted you should try and keep the dog upright and moving forward. So when I anticipate a dog is about to lay down on the ground one thing I might do is run a few steps forward with the dog to not let them.

- I might also keep a treat ready in my hand and lean down low and in front of the dog to keep it moving forward. I've even bought finger puppets at street fairs and used them to keep the dogs attention going forward. This philosophy is similar to human behavioral psychology where people change their normal approaches to something they are having problems with.

- Change the dog's rhythm. If they are used to walking 4-5 feet and then crouching down, get them going 9-10 feet and do everything possible to not let them crouch down. In the end it's better for the dog to get out of this habit and while this dog might not turn into your smoothest walk of the day, it might be one of the small victories you love and cherish.

Use equipment: You can use training equipment in combination with your checking and using your voice ("ahh, ahh, ahh"). Training equipment should not be a substitute to working on your dogs' issues, it should just make them easier to fix.

The equipment (for the dogs)

Becoming an expert on the equipment dogs wear not only ensures safety it will also increase the chances of your business being successful. Why is that? The equipment a dog wears can greatly influence the experience of walking it. If a dog wears the wrong equipment the walk can be worse and vice a versa. Your ability to recommend the right equipment to your clients might seem small but it could give you long lasting credibility with them.

You can't walk a dog unless you're familiar with the equipment the dog wears outside. If you show up at a client's apartment and you're not familiar with the apartment make sure to ask the client for help.

I don't think the use of equipment is something best described in writing or even through images. Instead I've created a section on our website where you can view video tutorials on the major equipments made for dogs.

You can find our videos on how to put on the equipment here: Go to *www.petsitterbible.com* > click the "videos" tab

Before walking a client's dog

Whether you have an extensive history walking dogs or not I'd *strongly recommend* practicing with a friends or neighbor's dog before taking on clients. Walking dogs professionally is much different than walking dogs casually. You need to know how to use different types of equipment and you need to be aware of safety hazards both in the homes and outside on the walks. Find someone who will let you practice getting equipment on their dog and walking on the street. This should be a low-pressure situation where you can work on things until you get it right.

Short but not tight

In cities you'll find a professional dog walker walks dogs short on the leash but not tight. The term "short but not tight" confuses some people so let me explain. You want there to be enough slack on the leash that the dog doesn't feel any pressure but short enough that you can protect the dog from city elements and if the dog is aggressive it can help you keep it away from other people and dogs. If you're too tight on a leash and the dog feels that tension you can make the dog feel like it's either doing something wrong or that there is danger ahead and it needs to protect you. In country areas professional dog walkers allow the dogs to be longer on the leash but I would still try and keep the dog to the left of your body and/or relatively short.

Encountering other dogs on your walks

Whether you're walking in the city or the country you'll likely encounter other dogs when on a walk. Encountering other dogs can be a great chance to socialize the dog you're with but it can also pose risks if the two dogs start fighting. When encountering another dog first look for signs in the person walking the other dog.

- Does the other dog owner stiffen up their body?
- Do they tighten their grip on the leash?
- Do they pull their dog to the side, out of your direction?

All of these are bad signs that obviously and likely hint their dog might have aggressive tendencies. What signs do you see in the other dog?

- Does it stop dead in its tracks?
- Does its hair stand up?
- Does it get low to the ground and start slithering like a snake towards your dog?

All of these are bad signs. What would be good signs in the other dog? Good signs might entail a smiling dog, like you're used to seeing in a Golden Retriever, with a gyrating body coming towards you with no hesitation. No matter what signs you see in the other dog or their walker, make sure to always ask the other person, "is your dog okay with other dogs?" And no matter their answer, still base it on your own feeling of the situation. If your dogs start to play and you start speaking with their owner, don't lose track of the dogs. Dogs can play nice for ten minutes and then one wrong move, like one dog smelling another's ear, could be misinterpreted by the other dog and a fight could break out.

What happens if a fight breaks out?

First of all you need to separate the dogs. Hopefully both dogs are on leash and you can just pull them away. But if you're in a dog run or if for some reason your dog is off leash, do *not* reach in front of your dog or the others dog's face in the midst of a fight. Your hand will surely get bitten. Grab your dog behind its back two legs and pull it away from the other dog. Check your dog to see if there are any open wounds. But no matter if you see open wounds or not get the contact information for the owner of the other dog. And check your dog ten minutes later because sometimes bight marks will not show up until minutes later.

Scavenging

Scavenging is when a dog tries to eat garbage out on their walks and a scavenging dog is called a scavenger. Scavenging is a very serious issues because a dog can eat things on the street that could get them sick or even kill them! Scavenging is more of a problem in a city than the country but no matter where you walk dogs you need to make sure your dog doesn't pick anything up off the ground. If you have a dog who is prone to picking things up off the ground you'll need to either teach it a command like "drop it" or put on a training device like a Gentle Leader. If your dog happens to pick something up off the ground you need to be on one knee in a split second. Grab the dog's collar with one hand and put your second hand to the back of the dog's tongue and scoop out anything in the dog's mouth. Don't waste a moment! On a city street there can be lots of items covered in Anti-Freeze, which for some strange reason is actually *sweet*. (But on a side note, I'm happy to hear there's a movement to bitter anti- freeze.) Just as dangerous though, could be a chicken bone or piece of plastic. Your best practice is to see ahead of the dog you're walking and avoid potentially dangerous situations. But if your dog happens to pick something up with its mouth pull it out immediately.

Looking at the ground

A good dog walker looks mainly ahead and periodically makes eye contact with and talks to their dog. An inexperienced dog walker looks down at the dog for the majority of their walk. This can be a mistake. You are there to protect the dog from getting into danger. You can't see these potential dangers if you're looking down at the ground.

Crossing streets/roads

Whether in a large city or a small town, crosswalks can be dangerous spots for walking dogs. In these times we're living, when people pride themselves on driving fast and having short attention spans, you need to take extra precautions to make sure you aren't putting your dogs in harm's way. Make sure things are obvious when crossing streets with dogs. Make sure there are no cars or bikes coming from any direction and don't *ever* try and beat a coming car with a dog in your hands. If the dog were to put on the breaks, squat down to start going to the bathroom, etc. you could be in some major trouble.

Avoiding light poles/electricity

Light poles are mainly an issue in cities but you might encounter some in small towns too. I would avoid lampposts and anything with electricity when walking a dog, especially on damp days. Unfortunately a few people and dogs have been killed in New York City from stray voltage. A woman was walking her dog in the East Village of Manhattan when her dog started to get shocked. She tried to help her dog and they both were shocked to death. I would just avoid anything that even might have electricity in it and on damp days I'd avoid any metal surfaces that are right next to electric poles (grates on city streets, etc.).

Should I take dogs to dog runs/let dogs run off leash?

Everything I've discussed up to this point details how to best control the situations your dogs are in. When you take a dog to a dog run or let them run off leash you lose that control. No matter how well trained a dog is there are primal instincts in dogs that can*not* always be predicted or anticipated. Here are some quick tips on dog runs and letting dogs run off leash:

- *Always* have permission from the owner of a dog before taking it to a dog run.

- Don't ever lose track of the dog(s) you're with at a dog run – don't read a book or turn your back and talk on your phone.

- If dogs are feisty in the run that day or if there are any fights I'd take your dogs out of the run – why risk it?

- If a fight ever does break out and you need to break it up *don't ever* grab a dog on the front of their bodies, towards their chest, mouth, etc. That's a sure fire way to get bitten – if your dog gets in a fight grab it behind it's back legs and pull it away from the crowd of dogs.

- Don't let your dog hump or be humped by other dogs – it's bad manners and some owners will get angry.

- If you are allowed to bring toys, balls, etc. bring a tennis ball and try and teach your dogs to fetch, it's one of the best possible ways to tire out a dog.

- A dog run is a good place to work on the "come" command to get the dog to run over towards you – some owners have a hard time getting their dog to come to them when it's time to leave – always have a treat in your pocket and let your dogs smell it as they pass by you in the run – when it's time to go and you call them over they'll think they're getting a nice treat.

- Make sure your dogs get their owner's money's worth – if your dogs don't run around or seem interested at the run maybe it's not a good place to take them – take dogs to the run for their benefit, not your enjoyment.

Socializing dogs

Socializing a dog is something you've probably heard before but what does it mean? It does mean what you probably think in having one dog socialize with other dogs but it also means a dog socializing in their environment. Dogs must

get used to their surroundings, the sights, smells and noises of the area they live. This can be especially important yet difficult when bringing a dog from outside a city into one. Some dogs can actually turn aggressive once brought into a fast paced city. Socialization for a dog, especially from a young age, is so important it can actually affect a dog's personality. A dog that is not socialized can be more timid, have less confidence and even turn aggressive!

There are many ways to socialize a dog without walking them alongside 7 other dogs. You can take a dog to the dog run. You can walk a dog with the same one or two other dogs every day and have them become friends. You can have play dates in a home between one or two dogs (make sure you test out these dogs together with the owner's home first and see how they get along). You can stop during your walks to search out other dogs to socialize with.

Not socializing a dog / leash aggression

Dogs who are not socialized or not allowed to socialize with other dogs can develop what is called *leash aggression*. Leash aggression in it's simplest form involves a dog wanting to reach another dog they see but is being held back by the leash that is attached to them. The beginning of leash aggression usually involves a dog barking at other dogs it sees while on walks. Over time this harmless barking and yearning to socialize with another dog while being held back might turn into aggression.

Aggressive dogs

Important: I do *not* suggest you personally try and figure out the issues of an aggressive dog. Dealing with aggression is tough enough for a seasoned dog trainer let alone a dog walker. What you can do is be aware of the signs of aggression in your dogs. If you see signs of aggression in your dogs you should direct the owners of those dogs to reputable dog trainers in your area.

Types of dog aggression

Here is a small list of some of the most common forms of dog aggressions:

- Fear/nervous biters.
- Dominance.
- Territorial (food, toys/balls, home).
- Predatory.
- Learned.

When dogs are aggressive with you/employees

Dogs who are aggressive with you or your employees are a big issue! You should not try and be a hero with aggressive dogs and you definitely don't want to put an employee in a position of getting injured by a dog. As I've already mentioned you want to involve a professional when it comes to an aggressive dog. Here are some common situations where you might experience a dog being aggressive with you:

- A dog that will not come out of its crate.
- A dog who hides in a corner when you try to leash him.
- A dog who tries to bite you when you try to leash him.
- A dog who tries to bite your hand while outside on a walk.

The equipment (for you and your employees)

The following are a list of items that will make your life outside much easier.

- *Blackberry:* I feel Blackberrys are the best cell phone for this type of job. Blackberry keyboards are extremely easy to type on and that's one of the most important features for someone on the go. They also provide very powerful business features like the ability to edit/create a word document or excel sheet. You can view cell phone reviews here: *www.reviews.cnet.com/cell-phones/.*

- *Shoes:* As you would imagine the shoes on your feet are extremely important in this business. When it comes to sneakers *I love* New Balance! The most recent versions from New Balance I like are:
  For men (and some women): New Balance Men's 587 & 993 Models
  For women: New Balance Women's 587 & 993 Models.

- *Gel insoles:* What makes amazing walking sneakers even more amazing? Gel insoles plus a good pair of walking sneakers make you feel like you're walking on clouds. I've only used Dr. Scholl's insoles and I've been very happy with them. You can purchase gel insoles from your local pharmacy or sports store.

- *Rainproof:* There's nothing more brutal for someone who works outside than to be rained on all day. What makes rain especially brutal is if it's also cold outside. I'd highly recommend investing in rainproof tops and bottoms.
  For men: The North Face Summit Series Men's Jackets
  For women: The North Face Summit Series Women's Jackets.

- *Feet, hands and face:* I feel the areas of our body we neglect when it comes to cold weather are our hands, feet and face. For your feet you want to wear light, breathable yet warm socks. For your hands I'd recommend using hand liners in addition to your gloves. If you walk dogs you want your gloves to be as thin as possible yet still warm. Why? It's very important that you're able to strongly grip your leash when walking a dog. For your face I'd recommend using a facemask on very windy days.

Safety equipment

At Downtown Pets I have made the safety of our dogs my primary concern. I have taken extra steps to do this by having all my walkers lock their leashes into carabiners worn on their wastes.

You can learn more about how we use the carabiners and additional safety measures we take on our website here:

Log on to *www.petsitterbible.com* > click the "videos" tab

End of chapter checklist

- Go to our website and learn how to use all the basic equipment for dogs.

- Get your own leash and an extra collar or two – put a few knots in the leash so you can grab underneath.

- Be aware of safety hazards that exist outside.

- Practice walking a friend's dog.

- Educate yourself on all the basics of dog training: teaching a dog not to pull, not put their butt on the ground a lot, house training a dog, etc.

- Have policies in place for what you do when something goes wrong with the dogs.

- Invest in quality clothing to walk comfortably outside.

Chapter 4

Working with Dogs Inside the Home

Inside the home

Dog walking is a unique job. It's a service job but you are serving both the dogs and their owners. Your clients will not see how hard you're working with their dogs but hopefully they will see positive effects on their dog. What clients will certainly base their opinion of you on is how they find their home and the daily requests they ask of you performed. One client might ask you to leave a light on in their kitchen at the end of the walk while another might want you to feed their dog everyday. Whatever the request might be and however unfair it is, some clients will base their opinion of you on how they find their in-home requests to be performed. If you forget to change a particular dog's water one day that owner might think you're a forgetful person. And if they think you're a careless person inside they will often think you are careless *outside* with their dog too. My point here is to take your clients in-home requests as seriously as the job you do outside with their dogs.

Some keys inside the client's home are (before the walk)

- Stop for a moment before entering a client's home and refresh yourself, maybe even close your eyes and get ready to walk this dog (bring the right vibe into each dog's home and walk – some dogs walk seamlessly while others can be tough on the leash - don't expect the dog who has a tough time to walk as well as your seamless dog – with some dogs you'll have small victories).

- If a client has a home alarm and you can't deactivate it call them immediately.

- Immediately upon entering an apartment make sure things look okay (make sure the dogs hasn't created a mess/gotten into trouble and also make sure the house doesn't look different than usual – we have actually walked into homes that were robbed and it was obvious).

- If a dog has gotten into some garbage make sure to inspect the garbage (is there any hard plastic that's been eaten? Any dark chocolate? Or anything else that might harm the dogs? If so call the owners immediately).

- Is the dog usually crated but you found it out of the crate? If so call the owners immediately.

- If you don't find the dogs home? Call the owners immediately.

- If the dog has at least 3 out of the following 4 issues: liquid stool, throwing up, low energy and no appetite, call the owners immediately. If the dog exhibits any one of these issues do leave a note that day about it.

- Gauge the temperature of the apartment, is it too cold or hot? (This can be a problem for any dog but if it's too hot certain breeds can get in real trouble like Bull Dogs, Pugs and French Bulldogs – but if it's a cold rainy day and then you find it freezing inside your dogs could sick).

- Do not get curious in the apartments. Don't look in areas you're not supposed to be (many clients have nanny cams or will be able to tell if you walk around their apartment – I wouldn't want my dog walker walking around my apartment, would you?).

- Upon finding the dog(s) give them some love, rub their chests, speak in a high-pitch voice and tell them they're a good dog (no matter how you feel that day give the dogs some love, concentrate on them and it will force you to leave your problems at the door and you'll do a better job).

- Grab some treats if there are any in the home and you're allowed to use them.

- Brush one of the treats past the dog's nose so they get a whiff and you *wake* them up.

- Put the dog(s) in a sit stay before putting on their equipment.

- Put them in a few sit stays before walking outside.

Some keys inside the client's home are (after the walk)

- Dry off the dogs if they get wet or dirty (if the clients don't have a towel designated for their dogs ask them for one).

- Change the dog's water after every single visit (fresh water extends the life of a dog).

- Enter answers into your sign-in book every day.

- If the dog is using wee-wee pads and has soiled any of the pads make sure to throw them out, *outside* the apartment.

- Never forget to feed a dog and if you're not sure if a dog should be fed and can't reach the owner, feed the dog – better full than hungry.

- If you need to put a dog back into a crate don't forget to and always try and open the door after you close it, to make sure it's shut solid (do the same thing for the clients' apartment doors, always try to open the door after you lock it).

- Do *not* explore the clients' apartments – stay as close to the entryway as possible unless the dog forces you farther in but don't pay attention to the clients' personal items, images, etc.

- Use the park ranger rule of leaving the place better than you found it – at the very least don't leave any sign of yourself in the apartment.

- Do *not* assume it's okay for you to eat in a client's apartment, go to the bathroom in a client's apartment or take a break in a client's apartment – many times it's not okay and if you don't already have permission don't do it.

- *Beware* of getting *too comfortable* in clients' apartments – don't start using their TV's, computers or ever opening their fridges – these are all easy ways to lose clients.

- Don't lose clients to mental errors in their apartments – if they want a light left on after a walk, or their dog fed, etc. don't ever forget to do it – the clients will often rate you on the job they see performed in their homes.

- Take pictures or video of dogs from your phone and email it to the client – they love that!

Warm days vs. cold days

The temperature on a given day might cause you to do the following:

- *Cold inside:* If it's too cold inside the apartments you might want to call the owners and ask them if you can turn up the heat. If a dog comes home wet it's especially important to dry them off on a cold day.

- *Cold outside:* When it's very cold outside, snowing, cold rain, etc. you might want to recommend a jacket for the dog if the owners don't already own one. In large cities they use a very abrasive salt to melt the snow on sidewalks. Once the snow melts it becomes absolutely brutal on a dogs' paws. You will routinely find a dog raising its paws on a bad salt day and at a certain point it becomes impossible for them to walk. There is a product called "Mushers' Wax" that can protect their paws from salt for the better part of the walk. You can also use traditional booties to protect their paws. Make sure to dry them off well with a towel when you get home.

- *Warm inside:* When it's too warm in the homes I'd ask the owners if it's okay to lower the temperature. You need to be especially careful with dogs like Bull Dogs, Pugs, Boston Terriers, etc. who have breathing problems. It can be a very serious problem if breeds such as this overheat. You also want to make sure dogs don't overheat.

- *Warm outside:* On a brutally warm or humid day you need to be very careful with dogs outside. You need to make sure they are hydrated and are not in direct contact with the sun too much. You also need to be aware of how warm the surface you're walking is that day. How do you check? Simply put your hand on the ground. If you can't keep your hand flat on the ground more than a few moments then it will also be hard for your dogs to put their paws on that surface. Again you need to be especially careful with Bull Dogs, Pugs, Boston Terriers, etc. who have breathing problems. You want to make sure your dogs are not overly exerting themselves. If a dog's tongue ever starts to turn purple you might have a major problem and should seek out medical attention.

Puppies

There might *not* be a more beneficial area for you to educate yourself in than puppy training. Puppies will routinely require the most attention, service and time of all the pets you service. With that said puppies also pose your greatest chance to make a profit.

When a client first brings a puppy home

A puppy will usually be at least two months of age when a client brings them home although I have seen dogs less than two months brought home. Keep in mind that most puppies will most likely have just been taken from their mother and had their world turned upside down. New puppies will be anxious, a little scared and many will experience *separation anxiety*. Separation anxiety is when the puppy experiences excessive anxiety regarding separation from their homes or from those whom they've developed an emotional attachment to. We discuss methods to deal with separation anxiety later in this chapter.

Puppy proofing a home

Puppies are similar to babies in that they will want to explore the client's home and they will want to put things in their mouths. Here are some keys to helping your client's puppy proof their homes:

- *Poisonous household item*: You will find a detailed list of poisonous household items later in this chapter.

- *Dangling electric cords*: Puppies love to chew things and if they chew on an electric cord it could be very dangerous. You can tap/staple cables to the wall if they are loose and you can store excess cable lengths behind furniture. Make sure dogs can't reach dangling cords and even spray some Bitter Apple on an unconnected cord to try and deter them. Bitter Apple spray leaves a nasty taste on those items a dog might chew. Hopefully after tasting the Bitter Apple they will not want to chew on it again. You can also unplug the cords in the area you section off for your puppy.

- *Keep your toilet lid closed*: A puppy playing in a toilet bowl can be a tough habit to break and the chemicals used to clean toilets can be harmful for them.

- *Balconies and decks*: Do not let a puppy wander unattended on a balcony or a deck.

- *Do not crate a dog with equipment on*: We'll discuss crate training later in this chapter but you should never put a dog into a crate with equipment on. If the dog's equipment got caught on the crate they could possibly hang themselves!

- *Section off an area for your puppy*: A puppy *can't* have free access to roam a home while the owner is off at work. The owner either needs to use a gate or crate to give the puppy a small and safe area to be in. If the owner uses a gate they might section off their kitchen or bathroom. If they use a circular gate/pen it would be best to position it away from furniture so they don't jump out of their pen.

Puppy vaccinations

Puppies need to be vaccinated to immunize themselves from diseases. Not all veterinarians believe in the same schedule for vaccinations but most puppies will receive three rounds of shots. Some of the common things these vaccinations will help protect against the puppy against are rabies, kennel cough and/or giardia. Kennel cough and giardia are found more in cities where large numbers of dogs interact with each other. How does a dog's vaccination schedule impact you, the dog walker?

- *Until fully vaccinated (avoid other dogs)*: Until a puppy is fully vaccinated you need to guard a puppy from other dogs out on walks.

- *Until fully vaccinated (avoid puddles/liquid)*: You can't allow dogs to lick puddles or any type of liquid on the street. Dogs transmit bacteria, and specifically giardia, through spit, urine, feces and throw up. When you bring a puppy home you should wipe off the their paws.

- *Still get outside if you live in a city*: Puppy owners in cities are often warned not to put their puppies freely on the streets until they are fully immunized. But you should still make sure to take a dog outside to get it used to their new surroundings. In the beginning, until they are fully immunized, you might want to carry the dog in your arms or a dog bag. It's important for puppies to get used to the sights, sounds and smells of their neighborhood.

- *Be in touch with the clients*: You and your employees need to be aware of where a puppy is in their vaccination schedule. You *can't* give a puppy free access outside until you know the puppy if fully vaccinated.

What is a crate?

A crate is a metal cage that helps you housetrain your dog. Here's a picture of a crate: *www.petsitterbible.com/images/dog_crate.jpg*

Before a dog gets crate trained

Before a dog starts getting house trained or if a client doesn't want to crate train there are other options to a crate. We've already discussed the idea of sectioning a dog off in a circular pen, bathroom with a gate or kitchen with a gate. You can still reinforce positive behaviors within these spaces. I would suggest putting a wee-wee pad on one of the sectioned off areas and as far away as possible I'd put a bed and their food/water. What does this setup reinforce? It begins to reinforce the idea of keeping your home and going to the bathroom separate.

House training/crate training

The method a puppy clients use to house train their dog will decide the daily walk/visit schedule they require. There is no better method to house train a dog than with a crate. Some clients will think it's cruel to keep a dog in a crate all day. Crate training is not cruel if the dog is walked enough. Dogs originate from wolves and if you're familiar with wolves, they sleep within dens. Dens are small confined spaces just like crates are. You need to do your best, without being pushy, to show skeptical clients the benefits of crate training.

Sizing a crate

There should be no more space in a crate then to allow a dog to stand up, turn around, stretch out and lie down. If a crate is too big the dog can hide in a corner after they go to the bathroom in the crate. In a properly sized crate the dog can't avoid a mistake if they go and that's partly how crates teach dogs not to go in the house.

How long can a dog be in a crate at a time?

Dogs should not be in a crate longer than their age in months equal to hours.

Examples

- A 2-month-old dog shouldn't be in a crate longer than roughly 2 hours between walks/visits.
- A 3-month-old dog shouldn't be in a crate longer than roughly 3 hours between walks/visits.
- A 4-month-old dog shouldn't be in a crate longer than roughly 4 hours between walks/visits.
- A 5-month-old dog and up shouldn't be in a crate longer than roughly 5 between hours walks/visits.

At 5 months and older a dog should not be crated more than roughly 5 hours at a time between walks.

How do you decide the walk/visit schedule for a dog being crated?

- *Age of the dog*: As we just discussed the age of a dog decides how long a dog can be in a crate between visits.
- *Find out when a client leaves in the morning*: You should base your first visit on the age of the dog and the time the client leaves in the morning. *Example*: If a dog is 4 months old and

a client leaves the house at 9am, you should arrive for your first visit between 12pm-1pm.

- *Find out when a client comes home at night*: Based on the same example we just provided, if a client comes home at 6pm, then their dog will require a second visit roughly 4 hours after the first visit, between 4pm-5pm.

If a client wants to crate train their dog they will need to have the dog walked/visited enough times in the day. If you have a client who wants to crate train their dog but doesn't want to pay for more than one visit you'll need to explain to them how that could be unhealthy for their dogs. Keeping a dog in a crate too long can lead to urinary tract infections and overall health issues from putting pressure on the dog's bladder. In the end if you still can't get a client to get enough visits to meet our formula above then I'd suggest your clients hold off on crate training. Advise the clients to wait until the dog will be old enough to only need one walk/visit a day.

What dogs should *not* be crated?

If a dog has a urinary tract infection or is having diarrhea they should not be crated. Why is that? A dog suffering from a urinary tract infection or diarrhea can't control their bladder and this defeats the purpose of crate training.

Here are some signs of urinary tract infections

- A dog drinking more.
- A dog drinking less.
- A dog constantly trying to go to the bathroom.
- A dog constantly trying to go to the bathroom and nothing coming out.
- A dog with foul smelling urine.
- A dog with blood in their urine.

If you think a dog has a urinary tract infection you should alert the owners immediately. All of the signs I mentioned can be serious but especially if a dog has foul smelling urine and/or blood in their urine. In a situation like that they should visit the vet immediately!

What dogs are hard to crate train?

Dogs purchased from pet stores can be hard to house train/crate train. Why? In the pet store they would spend their days going to the bathroom in their crates.

Introducing dogs to crates

It's important that a dog is slowly introduced to a crate and sees it as a friendly place. You might recommend an owner tie open the door to the crate the first time they use it. This way the dogs can come and go as they please. During the first day you introduce your dog to a crate I'd feed him inside the crate and again not close the door behind as he goes in. You should start to close the door behind the dog slowly through the day. In the beginning stay by the crate near the dog when you do this but over time you'll want to leave the room.

Dogs will whine for you: Dogs will whine at first when you lock them into their crates. Owners often mistake this for thinking the dogs hate the crate. But dogs are usually whining because they want to be near their owners, not because they hate their crates.

What's the major idea behind house training a dog?

The main idea is that the dog can't go to the bathroom in the home and it's just that simple.

To view additional resources on house training dogs please click the following article to learn more:

www.petsitterbible.com/house_train_dog.html

Some other keys to puppies

There are skills we have already discussed that will greatly help you working with puppies and they are:

- Teach puppies to sit, stay and come on command.

- Socialize puppies with their environment and with other dogs (once they have received their vaccines).

- Use your voice to let the dog know when you are happy with them vs. when they are not doing what you want. *Example:* Utter "ahh ahh ahh" in a sharp voice when a dog isn't doing what you want them to. But say "good dog" with a calming voice when they are doing something you want, etc.

When a dog will not come out from under a bed, out of a crate, etc.

A dog who is apprehensive to go out on a walk when you arrive can be a big problem, especially if you are keeping a tight schedule. Here are some tips to dealing with a dog like this:

- *Do not pursue the dog*: Pursuing a scared dog can lose their faith in you plus you might even make it so fearful it bites you.

- *Try and get the dog curious in you*: Go in the other room, or just sit down on the ground and turn your back to dog. They will often become interested in you when you show no interest in them.

- *Leave the house and come back in*: Sometimes leaving the house and coming back in can solve the problem all together. It's like you're clicking a reset button and starting all over.

- *Invite the dog to go for a walk*: Grab the leash, show it to the dog and walk over to the front door. Speak very positively and say, "come, let's go for a walk, come on." Make it seem pretty obvious you're going out for a walk.

- *Beard, glasses and hats*: Some dogs are afraid of these things so make sure you're not wearing a hat or wearing sunglasses if you find a dog to be scared of you. If you have a beard and find dogs often get scared of you, you might actually want to think about shaving.

- *Do not try and be a dog trainer*: You are here to walk the dog and help it with its problems but you are *not* here to be a dog trainer. If this dog is showing you teeth, growling or showing any type of aggression do *not* pursue the issue.

- *Meet with the owner a few more times*: A dog will accept you more if it sees that it's owner accepts you. So I'd arrange to meet with the owner a few more times and try and have your meetings start outside of the apartments. Go for a walk together, maybe even grab the leash from the owner in the middle of the walk and then walk back inside the apartment together. I find this to be a much more successful method than starting the meeting inside the homes.

- *Do not take this dog on group walks (not yet at least)*: A dog like this is not ready for a group walk and may never be. This dog might need the attention of an individual visit, at first at least.

Important: If you can't figure out how to get a fearful dog outside through these or your own methods, then involve the owners and recommend a trainer. Fearful and anxious dogs, but especially aggressive dogs are tough enough for a professional dog trainer to deal with let alone a dog walker.

Separation anxiety – barking

This is a very serious issue for you as a pet professional to figure out. For owners who live in a housing complex, a barking dog can get them complaints and anger from fellow tenants. If the barking is really bad a client can even be at risk to be evicted from their apartment. Here are some tips to working with dogs that experience separation anxiety and/or bark a lot:

- *Increased cardio*: The first solution to many dog issues is to increase their walk times for the day or at least to increase the pace on the walks. As the saying goes, "a tired dog is a good dog."

- *Increase the quantity of walks*: If the choice is one 30 minute walk a day or two 15 minute walks a day, go with the two 15 minute walks. If the choice is one 60 minute walk a day or two 30 minute walks, go with the two 30 minute walks, etc. Multiple walks have a better impact on the dogs than one long walk.

- *Increase stimulation in the homes*: Have you ever heard of a Kong? They are smart, little red rubber toys that you can wedge treats or food inside of. It takes the dogs some time to get the treats out and this grabs their attention for awhile. It might be good to give a dog who suffers from separation anxiety a Kong a few minutes before walking out the door (with the owner's permission of course). You might even talk to the owner about freezing ingredients inside of the Kong. This make it take longer for the dog to get the full treat.

- *Dog runs, dog running, playing fetch*: I haven't found anything to tire a dog our more than running with it. But you can't ask your daily dog walkers to run with a dog, you'll need to hire long distance runners to do this. If a dog likes going to the dog run and is active there it might be a good idea to frequent the local run. It would be especially helpful if you could get the dog to play fetch with you and a ball.

A dog who is barking might involve some of the following to correct it

- *A command to correct the barking*: You and the owners should come up with a command you use every time the dogs barks, like "ahhh ahhh ahh, no bark." And then when the dog stops barking, "good dog, good dog."

- *Something to startle the dog when it barks*: Some people take an empty plastic bottle and fill it with pennies. Whenever the dog starts to bark they shake the bottle to startle the dog and then use the correction of, "ahh ahh ahh, no bark." And when the dog stops barking, "good dog, good dog."

- *Understanding of dog behavior*: It's completely understandable for a dog to bark a few times at noise outside your front door. It's inherent in most dogs to do this actually and would be abnormal for them not to. But a dog who continues to bark endlessly has a problem that they need help with.

- *Everything mentioned for separation anxiety*: Most everything described in the separation anxiety section applies to a barking dog too, because the issues can be one and the same. Increased cardio and stimulation should help a dog with barking.

- *Involve a trainer*: If the issue is so serious the owner might lose their apartment you should involve a dog trainer. This issue is so serious that some owners will *get rid of their dogs* instead of dealing with the issue! So you want to make sure to put some special attention on issues such as this.

- *Buy a noise machine*: A noise machine will go off every time the dogs starts to bark. It will match the dogs bark and make a sound louder than the bark. This is the least successful probably of all the ideas but it wouldn't hurt and it might even help.

- *Shock collars/citronella collars*: I do not recommend using shock collars or citronella collars. They are painful and in my mind they don't even solve the problem.

Excitable peeing

Excitable peeing occurs when a dog, especially puppies, gets overly excited when someone comes home and uncontrollably urinates. It might not seem like a big deal but it is and it can actually effect a dogs ability to be house trained. Here are some keys to help a stop a dog from excitable peeing:

- Don't make eye contact with the dog for the first few minutes upon entering the dog's apartment.
- Don't speak in a high-pitched voice upon entering the apartment.
- Don't play with the dog before leaving the apartment.
- Get the dog out of the apartment quickly upon leashing them.

Elevators

Elevators can be precarious because there's nowhere to run if a problem occurs. If you are walking an aggressive dog or if an aggressive dog joins you in the elevator it could be a big problem. Here are some keys to elevators:

- Don't stand directly in front of an elevator door. You have no idea what stands behind the door as it opens. Stand back or to the side of an elevator door.
- When you step into an elevator put your dog to the back corner and stand between the dog and the door. This way if the elevator door opens and a dog comes running in you can block it.
- Do your best to avoid riding the elevator with strange dogs and wait for the next elevator if necessary.
- Put your dog in a sit stay when you get into the elevator.

Daily feedback

No matter how much contact you have with owners you should have a daily sign-in at their apartment. This way the clients can verify you were actually there. A daily sign-in book is also a great place to chart a dog's progress when it comes to house training, leash training or simply tracking their mood. It's also a good way to verify your billing at the end of the week if you can't remember. In our sign-in books we chart the services performed (1 x 30 minute walk, 1 x 15 minute walk, etc.) and we also chart the dogs behavior that day (went #1 and #2, was in a good mood today, found a mess when arriving, etc.). If anything happens with the dog that requires immediate attention I email or call the owner.

Some things that might require an immediate email would be

- Found a mess when arriving but it doesn't look like the dog ate anything dangerous.
- The dog threw up, had no appetite, had low energy, had a loose stool.
- Dog was limping.

Issues that might require an immediate phone call would include

- Blood in the urine; blood in the stool.
- An open wound on the dog; the dog is limping.
- The dog threw up and had diarrhea on the walk.
- The dog got into the garbage and it looks like it ate some hard plastic or anything on the list of dangers for dogs below.
- The owner's house looks like it's been robbed or things seem out of sort. You will obviously decide for yourself what is worth contacting an owner about and how to do it but hopefully the above will give you a framework.

Checking for ticks

No matter if you work in the city or country ticks can be a problem for the pets you work with. The following link will detail some of the keys we use to check the dogs we walk at Downtown Pets:

www.petsitterbible.com/checking_for_ticks.pdf

In-home dangers for dogs

Prescription Pills (human or pet)

Sadly, prescription pills are always high on the in-home danger lists for dogs. If you see any bottles of prescription pills that could be reached by dogs move them to a different location and leave a note telling the owners you did so.

Chocolate

If you believe your dog has eaten chocolate you need to call a vet immediately. Certain levels of chocolate can kill dogs. Chocolate with high cocoa counts are the most dangerous like cooking chocolates, followed by dark chocolate but milk chocolate and white chocolate can make a dog sick too. Symptoms of chocolate poisoning include vomiting, diarrhea, restlessness, hyperactivity muscle tremors, increased urination and increased heart rate.

Raisins

A large amount of raisins eaten at one time can be toxic for a dog and hurt their kidneys.

Alcohol

Alcohol can cause, vomiting, diarrhea, difficulty breathing and tremors. It can also cause death.

Hard plastic

Hard plastic can get caught in a dog's digestive track and can even lead to death.

Coffee and Tea

Caffeine can make dogs jittery, increase their heart rates and in certain cases even cause death.

Potatoes that are green

These can cause a bloody stool, trembling, and even cardiac arrest.

The following is the ASPCA's list of the top ten hazards encountered by pets in 2009

"For several years, human medications have been number one on the ASPCA's list of common hazards, and 2009 was no exception. Last year, the ASPCA managed 45,816 calls involving prescription and over-the-counter drugs such as painkillers, cold medications, antidepressants and dietary supplements. Pets often snatch pill vials from counters and nightstands or gobble up medications accidentally dropped on the floor, so it's essential to keep meds tucked away in hard-to-reach cabinets.

Insecticides

In our effort to battle home invasions by unwelcome pests, we often unwittingly put our furry friends at risk. In 2009, our toxicologists fielded 29,020 calls related

to insecticides. One of the most common incidents involved the misuse of flea and tick products—such as applying the wrong topical treatment to the wrong species. Thus, it's always important to talk to your pet's veterinarian before beginning any flea and tick control program.

People Food

People food like grapes, raisins, avocado and products containing xylitol, like gum, can seriously disable our furry friends, and accounted for more than 17,453 cases in 2009. One of the worst offenders—chocolate—contains large amounts of methylxanthines, which, if ingested in significant amounts, can cause vomiting, diarrhea, panting, excessive thirst, urination, hyperactivity, and in severe cases, abnormal heart rhythm, tremors and seizures.

Plants

Common houseplants were the subject of 7,858 calls to APCC in 2009. Varieties such as azalea, rhododendron, sago palm, lilies, kalanchoe and schefflera are often found in homes and can be harmful to pets. Lilies are especially toxic to cats, and can cause life-threatening kidney failure even in small amounts.

Veterinary Medications

Even though veterinary medications are intended for pets, they're often misapplied or improperly dispensed by well-meaning pet parents. In 2009, the ASPCA managed 7,680 cases involving animal-related preparations such as non- steroidal anti-inflammatory drugs, heartworm preventatives, de-wormers, antibiotics, vaccines and nutritional supplements.

Rodenticides

Last year, the ASPCA received 6,639 calls about pets who had accidentally ingested rat and mouse poisons. Many baits used to attract rodents contain inactive ingredients that are attractive to pets as well. Depending on the type of rodenticide, ingestions can lead to potentially life-threatening problems for pets including bleeding, seizures or kidney damage.

Household Cleaners

Everybody knows that household cleaning supplies can be toxic to adults and children, but few take precautions to protect their pets from common agents such as bleaches, detergents and disinfectants. Last year, the ASPCA received 4,143 calls related to household cleaners. These products, when inhaled by our furry friends, can cause serious gastrointestinal distress and irritation to the respiratory tract.

Heavy Metals

It's not too much loud music that constitutes our next pet poison offender. Instead, it's heavy metals such as lead, zinc and mercury, which accounted for 3,304 cases of pet poisonings in 2009. Lead is especially pernicious, and pets are exposed to it through many sources, including consumer products, paint chips, linoleum, and lead dust produced when surfaces in older homes are scraped or sanded.

Garden Products

It may keep your grass green, but certain types of fertilizer and garden products can cause problems for outdoor cats and dogs. Last year, the ASPCA fielded 2,329 calls related to fertilizer exposure, which can cause severe gastric upset and possibly gastrointestinal obstruction.

Chemical Hazards

In 2009, the ASPCA handled approximately 2,175 cases of pet exposure to chemical hazards. A category on the rise, chemical hazards—found in ethylene glycol antifreeze, paint thinner, drain cleaners and pool/spa chemicals—form a substantial danger to pets. Substances in this group can cause gastrointestinal upset, depression, respiratory difficulties and chemical burns.

Prevention is really key to avoiding accidental exposure, but if you suspect your pet has ingested something toxic, please contact your veterinarian or the Animal Poison Control Center's 24-hour hotline at (888) 426-4435."

Cat visits - exotic animals - birds - fish visits

Cat visits and any animal that doesn't come outside can be a relaxing break from running around outside. If a prospective client asks if you can take care of an animal you have no experience with be up front about your lack of experience. But more than likely they can show you how to handle the animal. Pets like birds, fish and exotics are often in cages or tanks and do not require handling the pet with your own hands. In regards to cats here are some basics I'd recommend:

- Clean the litter box.
- Clean the food bowl.
- Give fresh water.
- Give a brushing if there's a brush.
- Give them lots of love and attention – talk to them – people falsely think cats don't need attention but they do.
- Do *not* pursue a cat who is scared of you.

No matter the type of pet I'd have them fill out an application although you will need to make an application more geared to in-home care only.

End of chapter checklist

- Leave daily feedback for the clients in a notebook or custom sign-in book.
- Study what safety hazards exist within client's home.
- Have a system in place for if a problem does occur within a clients' home.
- Create a policy for yourself and your future walkers on how to treats a clients' home.
- Study methods to deal with shy, scared and anxious dogs that will not come out for a walk.

- Study methods to deal with separation anxiety and a barking dog.
- Come up with solutions *other than* a shock collar for your clients to deal with a barking dog.
- Become an expert on house training and crate training dogs.
- Know how long is allowable for a dog to be in a crate.

Chapter 5

Starting Your Pet Service for Under $1,000 – Street PR and Marketing

Street Level Marketing

Okay, maybe when you read the title of this book you were skeptical about being able to start a pet service for under $1,000? Well here you go, my game plan to start your pet service for under $1,000. Of course it will take sweat equity too but that comes with building any business.

Before we get started I want you to do one of two things:

- Take an existing credit card and from this point forth dedicate this card to be used *only* for expenses of your pet service.

- Or apply for a new credit card that you will *only* use for company expenses.

The benefit of using just one credit card for your business expenses is you can centralize all your bills for the business and that makes them easier to keep track of, organize, and search within. At the end of the year you'll be able to find almost all of your tax-deductible items in one place, on one card, etc.

Before you start walking someone else's dog

Bonding and Insurance...

Being bonded and insured is a common term in the pet services industry and a client expects you to be bonded and insured. But more importantly you need to be bonded and insured if you're going to be working with someone else's animals. Insurance protects you if something happens to or because of the pet you're working with. A liability bond protects you if someone working for you is convicted of robbing or damaging a client's home.

You have to get bonded and insured before you can walk someone else's dogs for money. If you were not bonded and insured and something happened to a dog you were walking, you would have no protection if you got sued.

To get bonded and insured you first need to be a member of either NAPPS (*www.petsitters.org*) or PSI (*www.petsit.com*). (-$100).

Once you are a member of one of these two you need to get pet sitting insurance:
NAPPS members: *www.petsitterinsurance.com/napps/liability.asp*
PSI members: *www.petsitterinsurance.com/psi/liability.asp*) (-$274)

and a liability bond:
(NAPPS members: *www.petsitterinsurance.com/napps/bond.asp* PSI members: *www.petsitterinsurance.com/psi/bond.asp*). (-$50)

Total Price: (-$424 a year)
Money Remaining: ($576)

Dog walking supplies

As a dog walker you'll want to carry your own equipment to walk the dogs and you should always have backup equipment on you too. The key equipment I'd recommend having on you is:

- 1 nylon leash (-$15).
- 1 adjustable collar (-$15).
- Biodegradable waste bags (-$15 a month).

Total Price: (-$45)
Money Remaining: ($531)

Getting the word out about your company

What's the use in becoming a professional dog walker if no one knows about it? You need to get the word out there about your company and here are three ways to do it:

- Business Cards/Marketing Materials.
- Word of mouth/Street PR.
- Establishing and maintaining relationships with referral partners.

Business Cards/Marketing Materials/Relationships

You never want to be caught without having a business card on you. With that said, you need to buy a business card holder and get some business cards. Business cards are a cheap, easy way to get the word out about your company. Unless you are an artist or know an artist I'm going to recommend you try Staples business card services. They are cheap, user friendly and provide free templates to easily create your business card templates. Do your best but don't try and create the Mona Lisa with your first business cards. You want them to be simple and descriptive. My present business cards say the following on the front:

Downtown Pets:
NYC Dog Services in Lower Manhattan 212.647.0634
clients@downtownpets.com

Don't write an essay on your business cards; just summarize what solutions you are offering for problems your clients will have and where you offer your services.

Staples offers a deal of $18.99 for 500 cards and they offer free business card templates. I have always had a good experience when it comes to shopping at Staples.

Estimated price with delivery: (-$29)
Card Holder: (-$25)
Money Remaining: ($477)

"Why do I rob banks? Because that's where the money is."

This is a famous quote from the feared bank robber Willie Sutton. But I want you to apply this idea to your street PR and marketing. Instead of trying to track down pet owners why not go to where they actually congregate? Dog runs, pet stores, vet offices, etc. Take your business cards and treats and a positive attitude to these spots and stand in front of them. They will be goldmines for you with prospective clients walking right by you all day. Keep this in mind as you read the following tips on getting your company's name out there.

Word of mouth

Building relationships is really the cornerstone of any business. Finding people in your industry, non-competitors and competitors, to receive referrals from could be one of the best sources of new clients you'll ever find. My relationships with dog trainers, vets and pet-store owners have easily led to over 100 client referrals and they were free!

Total Price: (-$0)
Money Remaining: ($477)

Name recognition as a new business in the neighborhood...

You know how in movies or TV shows the new neighbors go around giving homemade cookies to all of their surrounding neighbors to say hello? Well this is a great idea actually. People are always suspicious of the new guy on the block and now you are the new guy on the block—but we're going to change that by doing the following:

- Once your new business cards arrive break them up into small bundles, maybe 25 cards per bundle.

- Come up with some type of sweet treat to give out. Something like homemade cookies made by you, a store, it doesn't matter. People like cupcakes too (^_^).

- I want you to take your bundles of cards and cookies or cupcakes to all the local vets, pet stores, daycares, dog trainers, etc. in the area.

- Let them know that you're a new dog walker in the area, that you walk dogs professionally and safely and that you'd like to build a relationship with them.

There you go. All of the major players in the pet services industry in your area now know your name. Does that mean referrals will start pouring in? Probably not! But you've planted a seed you'll need to cultivate so they don't forget your name. We want all of these people to trust you and the idea of referring their clients to you. And when you do receive a referral from them? Take extra special care to make them happy so you keep receiving referrals.

Estimated Cost: (-$30)
Money Remaining: ($447)

Street PR events

Okay so now that you've planted the seed with the professional pet services in your area it's time to go after your clients. And what better way to engage your prospective clients than face to face? What I like about street PR events when it comes to the pet industry is that it's easy to see who your client is. If they're walking a dog they are a prospective client, pretty easy right? Again it doesn't mean there's a high percentage you'll hear from them because it's really a numbers game. You need to get your card into as many people's hands as possible and have as many good conversations as possible. A very small sliver of these people will ever call you but don't let that deter you. You will get clients from street PR but not always directly. Maybe you'll give a card to someone who doesn't need a pet sitter but refers a friend to you. Or maybe they tell the human resources manager at their office that you should be referred to everyone in their office for pet sitting. Or maybe you'll give the local new anchor in your town a card and they'll do a story on you. You never know where your handing your card to someone will take you. Just don't expect instant gratification all the time.

Jazzing up your street PR

These days, depending on where you live, we are all getting bombarded with solicitations on the street. For some it's like a form of spamming people. While most of these solicitations are for good causes, they usually involve requests for money, your time, etc. So instead of just handing out your cards on the street I want you to hand out dog treats with the cards. Go ahead and buy a nice big box of healthy dog treats. I'd highly recommend buying something vegetarian (Wellness makes a great vegetarian treat with banana, yogurt and honey). The benefit of a vegetarian treat is you don't have to worry about a dog's allergy to meat. Now with your business cards and treats in hand you are good to go.

The experience of doing street PR

I tell my employees to perform street PR in the following way:

- Find someone walking a dog on the street or coming out of a pet store, vet office, etc.

- Engage them by first acknowledging the dog. Ask the owner if you can say hello to the dog. Next tell them, "I'm from (your company name) and we're handing out free treats today." Next hand them a treat or two and your business card at the same time. If they don't have a dog just try and hand them a card.

- Don't ask them if they want the treat or business card. Hand them the treat and business card as you greet them.

- If they refuse the treat still try and hand them the business card and say, "hey well if you ever need a dog walker or pet sitter I do work in your area."

It's that simple. The key is to not give them the option of saying yes or no, to "hey do you

ever need a pet sitter or dog walker?" People don't like choices. People can get flustered with choices and often will prefer to get out of the situation than make a choice. Just get the card into their hands and tell them a quick snippet about you and your beliefs on walking dogs.

Estimated Cost: (-$15)
Money Remaining: **($432)**

Offering Referral Fees

Offering referral fees to people could be a good way to get new clients. I try and offer referral fees to people in the housing market and all its different areas including:

- Real-estate brokers: A real-estate broker might be renting or selling an apartment to a couple just moving into the area with their pet and they aren't familiar with any local pet services.

- On-site managers: On-site building managers (or attachés as they are sometimes called) help their tenants get used to the local surroundings. One of the items they help tenants with is the care of their pets.

- Movers: Movers are the first contact someone will have going to a new location. If the mover sees clients with a dog why not throw them a business card?

- House Cleaners: House cleaners are in the house weekly and know if the owners have a pet.

- Doormen and Supers: Doormen and supers have a personal bond with their tenants and know if they own a pet.

I mean, who better knows what's going on in the buildings in your area than these people? And like most people all of the above seem to be especially motivated by the chance to make extra money and especially easy money. Call up a local moving company or real-estate office and tell them you'd like to start a referral program with them. Maybe you'll pay $100 for each client who's with you more than 3 months. Whatever you decide just make sure you do have a number set in stone when you speak to them and don't offer too much. Keep in mind how much you might make from the client before offering a $500 referral fee.

What type of person is already in the homes of your owners?

- Doormen.
- Supers.
- Real estate brokers.
- Nannies.

Non-competing businesses in the pet service industry

- Dog trainers .
- Pet stores.
- Vets.
- Daycares.
- Dog walking and pet sitting businesses in areas you don't service.

End of chapter checklist

- Take an existing credit card or get a new one and put all your business expenses on that single card.
- Get bonded and insured before entering a client's home.
- Get some dog walking supplies.
- Order some business cards and buy a card holder to carry with you.
- Concentrate on vet offices and pet stores in your neighborhood.
- Bring some dog treats with you and do street PR in an area like you'd to concentrate on.
- Offer referral fees to non-competing businesses.

Chapter 6

How to Start a Pet Service for Under $1,000 – Your Company Website and Ranking Well on the Internet

Your Company Website – Google – Search Engine Optimization (SEO)

Creating a web presence and getting clients from the web:

There are 5 major ways to be found on the Internet and they are:

- Ad Words.
- Craig's List.
- Personal Website.
- Images / Videos.
- Google / Search Engines.

Ad Words

(*www.adwords.google.com*)

Ad Words are those sponsored ads you see appearing at the top of and to the right side of search results on all the main search engines (Google, Bing, Yahoo, Ask, etc.). Ad Words are the major way the search engines make money so there are lots of features available to help you understand how to use Ad Words and how to best optimize your ads. You can create an Ad Words campaign and be online within minutes of verifying your account. Click the Ad Words link above and learn more about the benefits of using ad words.

The downside to *depending* on ad words is that they cost money. If you don't optimize your website organically to place well on search engines then you're going to be held hostage to paying for Ad Words forever! I think the best solution is to invest in Ad Words in the beginning but as your company grows pull back your Ad Words budget as your natural search engine standings improve.

Also make sure to take full advantage of all the tips, tricks, and statistical reports that the Ad Word programs provide you. An Ad Word program's aim is for your ad to be successful (and that's not always the case with traditional print and commercial advertising).

Tip: I would 100% recommend using ad words to get started. At the very least they should help your website get indexed faster on the Internet.

Estimated cost: (-$35 a month budget to start)
Money remaining: ($397)

Craig's List

(*www.craigslist.org*)

Craig's List is one of the easiest ways to get new clients and it's free! That's right, you can put up an ad in their community section, under "pets" for free. Don't get me wrong, you're not going to build your entire company off free Craig's List ads but you should be able to get a few clients off it periodically, and again it's free. Some keys to using Craig's List are:

- Create a user account (this way you can repost ads once they have expired without having to create them from scratch).

- Use colored fonts in your ads (not too many or too crazy but small touches that will separate your from the other ads).

- Use images in your ads.

- Have your titles catch people's attention.

- Post every single day.

- Try and get a sense for what time of day you get the most responses for Craig's List ads.

- Set up a specific email address just for your Craig's List ads and this will help you get a sense of how many people you are getting from them.

Estimated cost: (-$0)

You might notice that I don't recommend advertising in print media (newspapers, magazines, yellow book, etc.). Is print media dead? No, but I have found for this industry most people will find you on the Internet. If you live in a small town I'm sure there are local papers and newsletters you might want to use. But in large cities and on the whole I would make sure to concentrate on the Internet more. The Internet is the way of the future for getting your word out.

Company Website – Images – Videos – Community Features

In this digital age, the majority of your prospective clients are going to come from the Internet. Your personal website will most likely be the first contact a prospective client will have with your company. With that said I would *highly* recommend that you create a company website. No matter how simple it might be, your website will be your number one marketing tool for your business and not having a website will put you at a major disadvantage. In the simplest terms the keys to your website are:

- It should be warm, welcoming and clearly state what you offer (services, area, specialties, etc.) right on your home page.
- You should have an "About Us" page to further tell people about your philosophies.
- You should have a "Contact" page where people can request service and or request more information.
- You should add images and videos from your daily walks.
- You should try and provide helpful resources for your visitors.
- Once you get a few clients you should get some recommendations to post on your website.

Creating Your Website

There are a few different ways you can go about creating your website, depending on your budget. You can:

- Hire a professional web designer and graphic designer.
- Hire only a professional web designer and do the graphic design yourself.
- Hire only a graphic designer and use a service like PSD2.html to transfer that graphic imagery into web standard code.
- Purchase a template for your website.
- Use a Blog as your website.
- Make a website yourself.

You can hire a professional web designer and or graphic designer

If you have the money to spare and can afford both a web designer (roughly $500-$1500 for a 5-10 page website) and a graphic designer (roughly $500-$1,000 to design the layout of your site: header, logo, font colors, header colors, some icons, etc.) then go for it. A great website gives instant credibility and is one of the best investments you can make for this and almost any business these days.

Place to find a web designer: You can post an ad on Craig's List and ask potential web designers to send you *links* to examples of their work. Have a budget in mind *before* you talk with anyone and make sure the designer knows your budget *ahead* of time.

You can hire a professional web designer and do the graphic design yourself

If you are artistically inclined you will be able to save a ton of money now and always on your website. If you are able to create content that is fitting for a website header, logo, etc.

then you'll just need to search out a web designer to help you with the rest. But please don't fool yourself. If you can't create art for a website (which is a very specific type of look) I'd be careful about being the artist for your site.

You can hire a graphic designer (or do the design yourself) and then use a chop site like PSD2.html to create the web content for you (website: www.psd2html.com).

Chop sites like PSD2.html take existing design layouts (an image/Photoshop file that mimics the look of your site with header, navigation bar, logo, etc.) and turns those images into actual code you can use on the Internet. The one issue though is that once you receive the code for the Internet you will need some understanding of how to edit it going forward.

You can purchase a template from a template website

I'm not a fan of this idea because I feel you are given the least control out of all the options and have rarely found layouts that I liked. If you do take this route I'd make sure you purchase a website based on a CSS style sheet.

Try this website out for web building: *www.psd2html.com/*

You can use Google's free website building program

www.sites.google.com

You can use a Blog for your site

Free Blog software like *Blogger* or *Word Press* provide simple ways to get a website online quickly and easily. Blogger in particular (by Google) is extremely user friendly, provides eye pleasing layouts but also gives you the ability to make simple changes to layout, font colors, font sizes, etc. But if you use Blogger I would still suggest hosting the Blog on your own server (your web host's server) and *not* Blogger's own. Why? Hosting your Blog on blogger will give your website an address like: WestVillageDogWalkers.blogpsot.com vs WestVillageDogWalkers.com. A web name without the ".blogspot" at the end is much easier for your potential clients to remember.

Blogger blogging software: www.blogger.com/start
Word press blogging studio: www.wordpress.org
Estimated cost for a blog (created by you): (-$0)
Estimated cost for a website template (edited by you): (-$25)
Money remaining: **($372)**

Create a website yourself

Creating a website for the first time can feel very daunting and can take up *a lot* of your time. Are there benefits to doing it on your own? Absolutely! Would I recommend it at this time? Not necessarily. At this time I would certainly learn the basics of web design, and we'll discuss some of those basics shortly, but at the very least I'd involve some type of professional (web designer or graphic designer) or use a Blog to get started. These will help you get off your feet quickly and can easily be updated, edited and completely changed over time. One of the benefits of getting online quickly is getting new clients but one of the other benefits is getting indexed by the search engines more quickly. We'll go over the search engines in more detail later in this chapter.

Important: You might think that your website should look the same on all of your visitors' computers but it might not! Each browser (Firefox, Safari, Internet Explorer, Opera) might display your website differently so *you need to test* your website on *each browser* to see how it looks. Internet Explorer seems to cause people the most problems and especially Internet Explorer 6. Just because your website looks right on your computer on the browser you are using, don't assume it looks right on your users' computers until you test it yourself.

Basics of Web Design

No matter what road you take in creating your website it is *extremely* beneficial to you, that you know the basics of web design.

CSS vs. HTML

To put it simply, HTML is the way websites used to be made and CSS is the way they are made now. If you work with a web designer I would make sure they know CSS and if they don't I would not work with them. What is CSS? CSS is a Cascading Style Sheet where the rules (font colors, font sizes, layout of pages, layout of header, logo, etc.) for your entire website are decided. What are the other major benefits of CSS, if you're not sold yet? When you use a CSS style sheet you can easily change your header, logo, navigation menu, etc. *So within 5 minutes you can change the entire look and feel of your website!*

Please click the following link if you'd like to learn more about CSS: www.w3.org/Style/CSS/learning

If you were to only know one thing about web design

I hope you become very comfortable with the basics of CSS and web design but at the very least you should know how to create links on your website. I'm sure you know what links are but to give you an example links usually look *like this* and when you click a link it takes you to another page.

How do you create a link?

A link can be created with text or an image but for now let me just show you how to do it with text. The basic code in a text link is:

<a href="*http://downtownpet.com*">nyc dog walker wesbite </a>

The result would be

nyc dog walker website

And when you'd click *"nyc dog walker website"* it would take you to the website you'd specified between the two quotes after <a href= in the code (in this case it would take you to *http://downtownpet.com*).

Links are essential on your website to help users navigate within your site but they are also helpful with referral partners. If you decide to exchange links with a competing business it's nice to be able to put its link on your site very quickly. There's nothing worse than needing to depend on someone else (a web designer, etc.) to create a basic link for you. It's a simple task but very important to know how to do.

Keywords in your text links

As a basic rule of thumb try as often as you can to have keywords in your text links. Google likes them and they are informative for visitors to your site.

Example

You have a page on your website dedicated to your "pet sitting services." You want to create links across your website taking visitors to this "pet sitting services'" page.

Option #1

Looking for a pet sitter? *Click here.*

Option #2

Please click the following link to learn more about our *pet sitting services*.

In "option #1" you have no keywords and the link is telling the search engines and your visitors nothing about what the page is about. But "option #2" tells the search engines what the page is about (giving your web ranking a bump) and is helpful for your visitors too.

The point here is to try and use keywords in your links specific to the services and products you offer. And to have your links be text based like the ones above and not image based. Image based link tell the search engines nothing about the page the link it's taking you to.

Another point about keywords in your text based links:

Try and have your keywords in your links truly represent the content of the page you are linking to. So the link we made above *"pet sitting services"* should be taking people to a page that discusses your pet sitting services. Search engines like this and again so will your visitors. Personally when I surf a site, if a link takes me to a site that has nothing to do with what the link has promised I usually leave the site very quickly. Don't lose your visitors faith!

Should I use Flash, or a Splash page?

Plain and simple: I would *not* suggest using either of these. They hurt your search engine ranking, and they will not even work for some prospective clients. When someone visits a site for the first time and a web page malfunctions, they usually are not going to try and figure out the problem. They would rather move on to another website, and you will lose their business.

Some common, and helpful pages to include are: "About Us" page

- Talk directly to the clients.

- Personalize yourself and the business.

- Talk about your experience with and love for animals.

- Link to your blog.

"Frequently Asked Questions (FAQ)" page

- Create this based on your responses to emails you receive from prospective clients.

- Not everyone will look at this page, but for those who do, it will save you time.

- Is a sign of professionalism.

"Client Feedback" page

- Post positive comments from clients who love your service.

- Ask clients who contribute to write these comments on a personal letterhead, to look more professional.

"Pictures and Videos" page

- Post new images and videos of the pets you service.

- Actively update this page.

- Clients love images and videos of their pets!

"Clients Info Page"

- Dedicated to all things for the clients.

- Holiday schedule/calendar.

- What's new.

- Images and videos.

Note: Web forms are an extremely helpful way to collect and sort information. I have found my online forms to be invaluable in screening new walkers and handling my client's schedule requests.

- The following is a link to my online form that potential walkers must fill out: *www.downtownpet.com/ACCOUNT.html.*

- This link takes you to the page where my clients can add services to their daily schedules: *www.downtownpet.com/add_service.html.*

You can learn more about forms on our website.

The theme/vibe of your website

The feel of your website is important both on a business level and a personal level. Obviously you want to love your website, be proud of it and love working on it but you also want your website to speak to the audience you are shooting for. And what audience are you targeting? Here are some different themed pet service website types I've seen online:

- *Icon/design based site/bright fun colors and fonts*: Sites like this have little to no photographs on them. They are based on colorful and fun icons, drawings, designs, etc. and have a fun, clean, and modern feel to them. While they can be super cute they can also sometimes lack the warmth and personality of a site mainly based on local images of dogs walking.

- *Professional studio images/black and white images/muted font colors*: Sites like this are usually geared to an older and wealthier crowd. I personally don't like sites like this because to me they seem old, dated and a bit cold. Instead of the frozen studio pose I'd like to see that dog running around at a dog run with other dogs. Again though it's up to you and there are many sites that go with this classic, old-school look. If your potential customer is older and very wealthy this might be the right look for you and your customers.

- *Point and shoot based images/bright and big font colors*: This is becoming the most common form of pet service websites. Images taken on the streets of the area you cover. People love the authentic and local feel of images like these and bright and fun colors go well with pet service websites.

Ways you can distinguish yourself on your website

No matter what theme you choose above, some of the best ways to distinguish your website are the following:

- *Logo:* A logo might become the signature image associated with your pet service, if it's a good and memorable logo.
- *Tag line:* What and where you service/what you specialize in.
- *Header:* Your header's size, shape, color and navigation within really sets the tone for the look of your entire site.
- *Navigation bar*: Your navigation bar (the main links for your site: home, services, about us, contact, etc.) is a part of your header but that doesn't mean it can't stand out. A cool navigation menu can make surfing your site more fun.
- *Font family:* The font family for your site (Arial, Georgia, Verdana, etc.) plays a big role in the feel of your pages. It's for you to decide what font-family is right for the vibe you're going for but keep in mind there are only a certain group of fonts that are guaranteed to appear on your users' computers.
- *Title fonts and colors*: Titles usually stand out from the rest of the text on the page and can be bigger, a different font, a different color and even have a different background color.

- *Rollover types*: Rollover types are for when you put your mouse over a link – there are different effects the link can have (change in color/added line/line disappears/image appears or disappears, etc.).

Adding Images to your Website

Once you've decided how you want to create your website you should quickly start thinking about the images and icons you'd like to add. Using images that are authentic to the area you'll service and of animals in general are extremely important. Early on in my company I licensed images from pet photographers that cost anywhere from $250-$500 each! And what was even worse I did not own the rights to these images so a competitor could have licensed the same images. I have since learned ways to add great images to my website that are cheaper and that my users have actually preferred! Here are some great places to get your images:

- *istockphoto.com (website: www.istockphoto.com/index.php)*: Istockphoto.com is a great place to find and license images for your website. For $15-$20 you can find really nice images to put on your website and part of what's so great? You get them the moment you pay for them, downloaded to your hard drive. On the negative side, some of the images can look "too professional" and you might lose the authenticity of being a local, personal business. My advice would be to buy images from istockphoto.com that fit nicely into certain pages of your site (example: themed pages, like a Christmas themed photo, etc.) but **not** to completely rely on them.

- *Use your cell phone camera*: Most newer cell phones these days have great cameras installed. If you're already walking some dogs I'd suggest you start taking lots of pictures of your dogs and other dogs you run into. That alone might solve your images issue and you will come up with lots of great, authentic and free images for your website. *One note*: Ask permission from the owners of the dogs before posting their images on your site and/or ask them to sign a release to use their images on your website. Some owners might not be happy if they find their dog's image on your website without permission.

- *Use a digital camera*: Digital cameras have gotten very inexpensive these days. I would *highly* recommend buying a nice, small, digital camera to carry in your pocket, either now or in the future. If you can't purchase one now ask your friends or family to borrow theirs. Run around for a few days and take pictures of dogs' faces, dogs being walked and also dog related places in your neighborhood (dog runs, vets, pet stores, etc.). I would also strongly recommend taking pictures of the area you service in general. Neighborhood specific images make the clients feel like you are a neighborhood company and people like that.

- *License images from professional pet photographers*: If you have the funds to do so and if professional studio photos fit the vibe of your site, then this would be the route for you. I would definitely make sure that "studio" images fit the vibe you are going for with your site though. If they don't these pictures will really stick out vs. the rest of the images on your site and they are expensive! To find professional pet photographers you can do a simple Google search of that term and you'll find plenty of photographers to contact. I would recommend trying to make a deal with them not to license the same image you purchased to anyone in your area. What a waste that would be if you spent $500 to license an image only to find your chief competitor using the same image. This is a concern in licensing images from istockphoto.com too but considering the images are so cheap it's not as much of a concern.

Going with istockphoto.com estimated cost: $75
Going with your own or a friends' digital camera: (-$0)
Money remaining (based on istockphoto.com): **($297)**

Icons on your site

Icons are a cheap and easy way to add images to your website. I would not completely rely on icons for your website; use images as well. Icons can add small touches of flair to key points on the page and look professional in general.

Estimated costs for icons: (-$30)
Money remaining: **($267)**

Organizing, editing and publishing your images

Working with your images

Now that you have your images you need to prepare them for your Website. If you don't already own a professional image editor let me recommend a great free one from Google called Picasa (*pc version: www.picasa.google.com/index.html# / mac version: www.picasa.google.com/mac/*). *Honorable mention for "free" image hosting:* Flickr *www.flickr.com/*). I would also sign-up for the online version of Picasa through your Google account online. Doing so will make it easier to share your images online and to create slideshows. *Paid version:* If you want to get a little more advanced with your images I'd highly recommend Adobe's Photoshop Elements. It packs all the punch of the very robust Photoshop software without the very high price point.

Sizing your images for the Web

There's a very big difference between sizing your images for the Web vs. for print. When you size an image for print you often want to make the image as big as possible to give you the very best quality. But images on the Internet do not and should **not** be large files. If you put huge image files on your website they will either spill way off the page and/or be so big they can't even load on your user's page.

How do you size an image?

In whatever image editor you decide to use there will be the option to size your images. Print size comes in inches (*example*: 8in x 6in) whereas for web images you're more interested in the pixel resolution (*example*: 1200 x 400). Most website widths will range between 800-1000 pixels. So based on that you should size your images accordingly (*example*: an image with a 250 pixel width will take up roughly third to a fourth of the page, etc.).

Choose the file format

You have two file formats to choose from, .jpg and .gif. Never choose .tiff for images on the Internet. I personally use the .gif format as often as possible as I find it maintains the best picture at the smallest file size and that helps your web pages load faster.

Add wording or effects

It can look very cool and professional to add a drop shadow, fade and/or words on top of an image. In addition to looking professional it will also allow you to promote ideas. Maybe you'll use a Christmas themed image of a dog walking in snow and add words to the side like, "Try our holiday services."

When sending images in emails

One of the benefits of using Picasa online is that you don't have to send people the images directly and have to worry about the file size etc. With Picasa online you can create a photo album and simply send someone the link to that album. If you do happen to email someone images directly make sure the files sizes are small and/or to compress the image beforehand.

Estimated Cost for image editor (Picasa): ($-0)
Money remaining: ($267)

Adding videos to your site

The prices for video cameras have become very cheap. It's now possible to shoot great web videos for $200-$300. Clients love videos of their dogs and videos on your website will look very professional. Even cell phones are starting to come pre-installed with video cameras. Here are some keys on video cameras:

- *Your Cell Phone (free)*: These days your cell phone can also stand in as your digital camera and video camera too! While cell phones might not yet produce stellar video footage, it should be more than adequate for web content and that's all we're really worried about anyway. I'd recommend making it a priority to have a good camera and video recorder on your next cell phone.

- *The Flip*: My brother recently came home with a Flip video camera and I was able to see how well it worked. It's a tiny little package but takes very legitimate video and still pictures. I do worry about image stabilization on smaller video cameras in general (chance picture will not be clear when camera moves around). I would try and have dogs walk toward you as opposed to walking alongside dogs as you shoot video and always hold the camera as still as possible as you shoot.

- *HD Video Camera*: If you want to make a full investment in digital video you can buy a very decent HD camcorder for $400-$600 but keep in mind you will also probably need to invest in accessories like a bag, batteries and tapes (although some HD cameras now shoot to an internal hard drive). You can find reviews on hd camcorders here: *www.cnet.com*.

- *You Tube (view website: http://www.youtube.com/)*: You Tube is the place where you can upload your videos once you've shot them and put them onto your website. What's so great about You Tube? You Tube provides a video format that will work on just about anyone's computer. It doesn't matter if they have a PC or Mac, updated software or not, You Tube should work on most peoples' computers. And that is not the truth for all other video formats. You Tube is also a community website and if you get a loyal following there it could reach thousands if not tens of thousands of viewers.

- *Vimeo (website: www.vimeo.com)*: Vimeo offers both a free video upload like You Tube but also offers a paid option where you can upload HD videos. Vimeo has a very cool look to its videos but I personally have had better luck with my You Tube videos loading faster.

- *iMovie (on Mac)*: iMovie comes free on Mac computers and is a great way to import your videos from your camcorder onto your computer. From there you can edit and or export to Internet ready QuickTime videos.

Using a friends' or your own video camera = (-$0)
Money Remaining: ($267)

So, I have created my website, now what?

The first thing you need to do is name your company if you haven't done so already and purchase your domain name. We will discuss the impact of your company name later in this chapter.

After naming your company you'll need to put it online. To do that you'll need to sign up with a web hosting company. For a website of this size, you will really not require much. But be wary of a deal that sounds too good to be true! Web hosts that offer you endless amounts of bandwidth and disc-space aren't necessarily lying to you—but they simply might have too many clients for the amount of servers they host. This would cause your website to sometimes run very slowly, or even be off-line. You want a web-host with a good customer support option located in America. And you should also go with a web-host you can pay month to month. In the beginning, I would definitely not suggest getting locked into a long- term contract with your web-host. In fact, you should try and find a web-host that has a refund policy in case you are not happy with your service after the first month. Once you start with this company, email their customer support (even if you do not have a real question you need answered) just to see how quickly they respond. The customer support of a web- host should follow up the same day, or at worst, by the next morning.

In regard to recommending a web host all I can say is I've been very happy with my web host, Pair Networks (website: *www.pair.com*). I don't think I've ever had a problem with my website being online and running fast and aren't those the most important things when it comes to your website? I have also been very impressed with their customer support. When I've emailed my questions they've usually been answered the same day and have provided very helpful resources. As a side note they also have a green policy and are carbon neutral, which I appreciate.

FTP Software

FTP software is software you use to upload your web files onto the Internet. As you make edits to pages, you'll want to republish them onto the Internet. Treat yourself to a paid FTP software with nice features like the one I mention below.

Paid (for Mac): Fetch: www.fetchsoftworks.com
Free: your web hosts' own FTP (usually much more clunky than nice paid versions)
Free 2nd option: Firefox' free Ftp software: www.fireftp.mozdev.org

Social Networking

Social Networking might be an overused term these days but the concept is now the industry standard for dynamic websites. You want to give your users the ability to give feedback. This feedback might come directly to you about your company or it might give them the ability to

comment on a list of vets in the area you posted. Social sites also involve blogging, images, videos, chat rooms, etc.

Here are some easy and "free" ways to add community features to your website

- *Start a Twitter Feed (website: www.twitterfeed.com/) and Twitter account (website: http://twitter.com/):* Twitter is a great place to condense all the new things going on in your company. When you make new posts your followers will receive emails with your new posts *automatically.* You can also put a live Twitter feed on your website where users can view all your recent Twitter posts. I'd check and see if your company name is available as a *user id* on Twitter.

- *Google Friend Connect* (website: *www.google.com/friendconnect/*): Google offers free software you can add into your web pages giving clients the ability to comment, rate and discuss items on your website.

- *Facebook (website: www.facebook.com/):* In full disclosure I am not an active Facebook user. I do not have my own personal Facebook page and I rarely use the company page I have. But there is no denying that Facebook is on fire these days. On Christmas Day 2010 Facebook surpassed Google for most visitors on the web that day. That's impressive to say the least and with that many people logging onto Facebook I would definitely try and utilize a page on it.

- *Disqus* (website: *www.disqus.com/*): Disqus is a free "comments" software you can add into your web pages. It is a little bit more flexible than Google's Comment and Rating Software and also allows users to have their reviews shoot straight into their Twitter accounts, etc.

- *Vanilla discussion boards* (website: *www.vanillaforums.org/*): Vanilla is a wonderful open source discussion board you can add to your website. It has a lively user community who come up with useful add-ons for your forum. This software does require the ability to edit CSS and PHP files. If you don't know how to do that you could probably find someone to configure a forum for only a few hundred dollars.

- *Mobile blogging:* Just imagine if your client goes away on a sleepover and they'd like some feedback on how their dog is doing and what do they receive? A video of their dog at home lying on its back in ecstasy as its tummy gets rubbed. You can rest assured the client will now rest easy and again this shows you are digitally connected and that will impress clients.

Cost: (-$0)
Money Remaining: ($267)

What to be careful about when it comes to community features on your website

Well first off is the concern about one or two bad apple clients talking badly about your company. You can limit this chance with the ability to monitor comments and force them to be pre-approved before going live on your website. But even so if you monitor too much you might alienate some clients who simply want to air issues they have with your service. So it's a slippery slope. I personally would recommend giving your users the ability to comment on things like local vets and pet stores but not your own company.

Another concern with relying too heavily on third party software and websites is that things might get confusing for your users. Why do they need to visit your Facebook page to learn about what's going on in your company. Why not have a page on your website dedicated just to client issues? Don't go too far off the reservation and your site when it comes to social networking sites. Don't just use them because they seem cool and popular. Use them if they answer an issue you are trying to solve, like consolidating information in one place, or wanting to use a site that takes care of all the image and video uploading for you.

Google/Search Engine Optimization (better known as SEO)

Search Engine Optimization is a marathon not a sprint

First off let me say that nothing is guaranteed when it comes to SEO and anyone who promises you top rankings is someone *not* to be trusted. Promises to quickly get your website #1 ranked on Google are either not true and/or they will lead to getting your website banned from Google. To be banned from Google can be death for a company. I will provide you some brief recommendations on things that should help your rankings on search engines and also provide some resources for you to read and blogs to follow. But if I can give you any advice it would be to make your website as informative and helpful as possible. That is probably the best roadmap you can take.

To start

If you want to place well on Google and search engines in general it might best to know what they like, right? Here are some very helpful and free resources to learn more about what Google likes:

- *Google's webmaster tools (www.google.com/webmasters/tools/)*:To utilize Google's Webmaster Tools you should do two things. First you should register your website within webmaster tools. Secondly you should *add a sitemap* for your website. There is a tutorial on how to do both these things. Once you've done these two things you can take advantage of all the advice the tool will give you on improving your site for your users and Google.

- Google analytics (*www.google.com/analytics/*):Sign up with Google Analytics and they will give you step by step instructions on how to add their features to your site. With Google Analytics you'll be able to understand how, when and from where visitors are finding your website. Based on this information you can optimize your web pages for the most popular search terms and title tags (title tags are within the code of your web pages and are found toward the top of the page – they tell Google and your visitors what this particular page is about).

- *Google's own blog (www.googleblog.blogspot.com/)*: Who better to listen to about how to place on Google than Google?

- *Matt Cutts' blog (www.mattcutts.com/blog/)*: Matt Cutts is an engineer at Google and his blog is famous for offering helpful advice for web masters.

- *Yahoo site explorer (www.siteexplorer.search.yahoo.com/)*: Yahoo Site Explorer allows you to view who is linking to you and it also allows you to view who is linking to your competitors!

- *Xinu (www.xinureturns.com/)*: Xinu is a very simple resource where you add your websites's url and it churns out a host of helpful information about your website.

What's in a name?

The name of your company can mean many things to you. It can be a cool sounding name with deep meaning to the core of your company. Or it can be a name that optimizes keywords and increases your ranking on search engines. So take a moment and think about what services you plan to offer. Dog walking? Pet sitting? Puppy care? House training? Dog Running? Nighttime walks? Weekend walks? Group walks? Individual walks? Do some Google searches for those services in your area and as an example I will search for dog walking in "NYC." Some of the different ways your potential clients would try and find you are:

- nyc dog walkers.
- dog walker nyc.
- dog walking nyc.
- nyc dog services.
- nyc dog walk.

Note: You'll notice that I didn't capitalize any of the search terms and you don't need to either when you search on Google.

Now if offering dog services in NYC were your main business you would notice the most common three words in the searches above to be NYC and Dog. Now try some searches on Google for other services you'll be offering and in the neighborhoods you'll be covering. After the results appear for each of your searches look on the bottom of the page. At the bottom of each search page on Google you will also find other common search terms people are using to find your type of business. What is the significance of this? The wording and order of words people use to search on the Internet might surprise you. If your pages don't show up for these search terms people will never find you.

What words are people using to find the services you offer?

I want you to sign-up for the free one-week trial at Word Tracker. Word Tracker is one of the largest "keyword research tools" on the Internet. Word Tracker charts what people are searching for, how often they are searching for it and how many other websites are competing for a single search term (like "moppy town dog walker" etc.).

Wordtracker (Free Trial) www.wordtracker.com

Two notes

- Please make sure to email yourself the results of your searches so you have them on file.

- Please make sure to cancel before the 7-day trial ends unless you plan to keep using it. Though for this business I don't see any reason you'd need it more than the 7 days.

Naming your company

Okay, so now you've done your research on Word Tracker and

you've discovered that the most common search term being used in NYC is "nyc dog walker." What can you do with this information you might ask? This information can help you decide what to name your company (unless you use a unique name) and it can help you decide what title tags to use on your pages.

We all have the urge to come up with the coolest names for our company but take some time to think about how important your website name is when it comes to Google. Having the search terms people are using to find your type of business in the domain name of your company is huge. If your company is called NYC Dog Walker and your website address is *www.nycdogwalker.com* there's a good chance you'll rank number one for that search term on Google. So seriously consider naming your company with your Google ranking in mind. I have three companies, the first being Downtown Pets, the others are NYC Puppy Care and NYC Dog Runners. Suffice it to say NYC Puppy Care and NYC Dog Runners rank number one for their searches. While Downtown Pets ranks number one for many Google searches and at least in the top 3 for almost all the major ones that's only due to the exhaustive work to keep it there. You can avoid a lot of this work by just naming your website with your key search terms. Does this mean you can't rank number one for search terms with the keywords in your domain? No, you definitely can but if you have competition from others with keywords in their website names it will be much harder.

Where to search for and purchase your domain names: www.pairnic.com/
Estimated cost to purchase a domain name (from PairNic): ($19 a year)
Money Remaining: ($248)

Trends I see in Search Engine Optimization

- *Name of site*: As we've already discussed the name of your site can play a big part in your web rankings.

- *Content of page*: Having the content of your pages be similar to the names of the page it's on plus similar to the name of links that point to it (as we discussed earlier in "keywords in a text link").

- *Title tags of pages*: Every web page has a "title tag" that tells search engines what the page is about. When you are on a page you can view the "title tag" content on the top bar of your search engine. Make sure that the "title tag" for each "individual" web page is specific to the content on that page (*example*: a page about "nyc dog services" should have "nyc dog services" in the title tag).

- *Quality of incoming links*: Incoming links are links from other sites pointing to yours. Search Engines like the *quality* of these sites linking to you more than they like the *quantity* of links pointing to your site. A high quality link would be a college, well respected site like the New York Times, a non-profit site, etc. Receiving a link from a site that breaks all of Google's rules does nothing to help your ranking and linking *to* a rule breaking site can actually hurt your ranking! For what Google likes and dislikes refer to their Webmaster Tools (*www.google.com/webmasters/tools*).

- *Don't worry about page rank*: You might hear people talk about *page rank* being important when it comes to the ranking of your site. Personally I would *not* worry about your page rank.

- *Be an information hub for your visitors*: Having your website be a place where people come to find a good local vet, or look at all your great pictures or read a witty blog post is good for your business and your web ranking.

- *Add images and videos*: Your users will love images and videos and so will the search engines! Make sure to use neighborhood names in your title tag for images (example: for a West Village dog walker make sure to put West Village in the title tag).

- *Title tags/not meta tags*: Google themselves have written that they do not pay attention to meta tags (to combat word stuffing). But they do look to the titles of your web pages to tell them what your page is about.

- *Zip codes and area codes*: Put the zip codes and area codes you service somewhere on a page on your website. Local search is the way of the future and in the future the following are the ways you will be found:
  a. west village dog walker
  b. dog walker 10014
  c. dog walker 212.

To get your website listed on the Internet there are a few different things you want to do

The following are all free

- Register with DMOZ (*www.dmoz.org*).
- Register with Yahoo (*www.siteexplorer.search.yahoo.com/submit*).
- Register with Yahoo Directories *www.ecom.yahoo.com/dir/submit/intro*).
- Register with Google (*www.google.com/addurl*).
- Register with Bing (*www.bing.com/docs/submit.aspx*).
- Yelp (*www.yelp.com*).
- City search (*www.citysearch.com*).
- Yahoo local (*www.local.yahoo.com*).
- Google local (*www.google.com/local/add*).
- Technorati (*www.technorati.com*).

Getting creative with Search Engine Optimization

Once you have done all the basics of getting your website listed you can think about raising the bar. The main goal of an SEO campaign is to get more people to link to your website or at least to get some well respected website to link to your website. How can you accomplish this goal?

- *Information resource:* On Downtown Pet's website we have lengthy resources on local vets, pet stores, animal welfare resources and local animal laws. We also have very detailed resources on house training and leash training. These resources have helped us become more than just a dog walking and pet sitting website. We have become an information hub where visitors return numerous times for different types of information. And how do I know this? Through my statistics on Google Analytics!

- *Get in the news:* This is not always something you have control over. But if you happen to get in the news this type of exposure can be good for your website if other websites link to you.

- *Get interviewed for an online article:* These days lots of papers and magazines are writing articles about the pet services' industry. If you get interviewed by someone you should ask if it will be put on their website and if so if you can have a link to your website.

- *Become an authority on a subject:* We have received a lot of links for our resources on house training. If you can become an authority on a subject it will attract lots of links to your sites.

- *Become an active blogger:* Search Engines love fresh, relevant content. There's nothing better for producing active content than on a blog. Just make sure you post a few blog posts a week.

- *Comment on other peoples blogs:* You might want to think about posting on other people's blogs. If you leave good points people will click your user id and that will take them back to your website.

- *Dynamic project:* What's a dynamic project? What if you create a small online video game that involves pets? Imagine if it becomes very popular and everyone wants to play the game. It gets so popular they even spotlight it in newspapers and on the internet. This might be an expensive project but it could bring you a bump in your web rankings, it could be well worth it. This is just an example of a project you could do. The point is to create something useful, fun or eye catching that brings attention and links to your website.

Resources

You should never stop learning when it comes to SEO because SEO will never stop changing. I find the following magazine and website to offer a lot of helpful hints:

- *Magazines:* Website Magazine (*www.websitemagazine.com/content*).

End of chapter checklist

- Start using Google's Ad Words.
- Create a Craig's List account and start posting free ads in the community and services' section (try and put images and fun colors in your ads).
- Build a website or a blog.
- Name your company.
- Choose a web host.
- Add images and videos to your website.
- Learn the basics of Search Engine Optimization (SEO).
- Use Google's Webmaster Tools and Analytics programs.

Chapter 7

How to Start Your Pet Service for Under $1,000 – Email, Billing and Your Office

Office Software and Work Area

The setup of your office workspace is extremely important both in regards to the experience of your clients and more importantly for yourself. When I say workspace I mean your digital and physical areas. Some keys to your workspace are:

- Being digitally connected through email, both on your computer and cell phone.
- Creating a system to file, sort, and search information.
- Creating a system to receive reminders about daily events.
- Understanding the basics of your computer and cell phone.
- Tracking, invoicing, and getting paid by clients.
- Paying your employees/reporting payroll.
- Creating a comfortable workspace to work in.

Update your Operating System, Browser and Software

In the following sections you'll find a bunch of recommended software to download. Before downloading all these applications I'd highly recommend that you update to the most recent version of your operating software (Windows Vista, 7, Mac OSX, etc.) and browser (Firefox, Internet Explorer, etc.). By updating to the most recent versions of these you will best ensure compatibility with the software you download. Once you've updated both of these, restart your computer to make sure the changes have taken place.

File structure on your desktop

After updating your browser and operating software it's time to create a desktop icon for your new company. If you haven't yet named your company just call it something specific like "dog walking," "pet sitting," etc. (to create a file on your computer's desktop usually you just need to right click on the screen > click new > click folder). Once you've created a company folder on your desktop open the folder and create sub-folders within that main folder. Some recommendations of sub-folders are:

- Images.
- Website.
- Downloads.
- Forms.
- Training.
- SEO.

These are just suggestions but my point is to make a main folder on your desktop for your company's information. Within that main folder make sub-folders to add important information. Your ability in the future to find things quickly will save you tens upon tens of hours of wasted time. Keeping an orderly file structure on your desktop will make less clutter, will allow you to enjoy your time on your computer more, and will make your time more productive. Take the time at least once or twice a week to clean up your computer's desktop.

Go with Google my friend

It's pretty amazing but you can get almost every type of software you'll need for your company from Google... and they're all free! If you haven't already, go to *http://google.com* and create a user account on the top right of the screen. Having a Google user account will allow you to use the following free apps:

- Gmail (for email).
- Google Calendar (for calendar event reminders).
- Google's Open Office (free word processing and data entry software).
- Google Docs (a free online network to track and document information).

And you know what? All of these are great software! And even better, many of these software sync with each other to make your life even easier. If you get an email in Gmail you have the option of clicking within that email and creating a calendar right in Google Calendar! This might not get you excited at the moment, but the more I describe it and as you start using it you should see how user friendly it is.

Paid versions: If you already have Microsoft Word or Excel on your computer I'd recommend just using them and skip downloading "Google Open Office."

Email

I can't stress enough how important your email program is when it comes to running this business. It's literally the origin of all the information you will process in the company. Most of your new clients and new employees will first contact you through email. Most of the problems you encounter, billing disputes, questions about service, etc. will be performed through email. We just happen to be living in a digital society and while speaking on the phone is great for certain areas of your business, you need to be email connected to do business these days.

Gmail

Gmail is a powerful and free email application that I would recommend you start with if you aren't already comfortable and happy with your email program. Gmail has a strong spam filter and provides lots of helpful features like: you can create your own rules to handle emails (sort them into certain folders based on the sender, delete them based on the sender, etc.); the ability to easily view past emails you've exchanged with the sender without having to search your entire folder of old emails; plus interactive features like video chat and others.

Your Website's own Email

Pretty much all web-hosting plans come with a certain amount of emails allotted to your account (200, 300, etc). The benefit of using your own website's email over Gmail is it does look professional being able to email someone with your company's name as the extension in your email address (example: *info@YourCompanyName.com*).

One idea might be to use a combination of both your own emails and a Gmail address. You can use your own email for new clients and with referral partners but use Gmail when a client signs up with you and going forward. The point is to try and use Gmail for areas of your business where you will need to track lots of information, remember past conversations, etc.

Some Email Keys

- Create folders in your email program to sort different types of email. For example in my email address for prospective clients I have a folder for client applications. If I'm looking for an old application I just open that folder and search for it.

- Tend to your old emails. As powerful as email programs are getting for searching within results, you should still periodically delete emails that don't detail schedule requests, complaints, etc.

- Gmail's "more actions" feature: When viewing an email in Gmail you can click "more actions" and some powerful features will pop up. The most useful of these features is the "create event" option that allows you to immediately create a calendar event on your Google Calendar and set up a reminder. Another powerful feature is the "add to tasks" option. When you click this for an email you'll view a link to this individual email on the right side of your page.

- Use signatures. Signatures are pre-written responses to questions you might receive a lot. What are your prices? Do you service my area? Can I get an extra walk this afternoon? Instead of writing the same answers over and over again create custom signatures that answer your most common questions and create signatures to sign the bottom of each email (your name, phone number, website, etc.). This is a sign of professionalism but again it will also save you tons of time.

- Use the rules features: Different email programs have different names for this option. In Gmail it is called "filter messages likes these." This is a very powerful feature you should get used to. In essence what you're doing is creating rules for what your email program does with certain emails. Let's say you want to filter all emails from a certain client into a folder, you can accomplish that in rules. Let's say you're receiving very tricky spam from a company who always says the same things in its emails but routinely change the email address they spam you from. Sure you can block each email every time but that's exhausting. Why not just create a rule that says every time you receive an email the words "great downtown deal" it should immediately be deleted? Now that would be easy. Play around with the rules and you can get creative. I now have a copy of every message that I send to my employees' cell phones also forwarded to their personal email addresses. This was created in case any of them misplaces it on their phone they can just check their email account.

- Assign categories to your clients. For now if it's just you in your company, categorize each of your clients as (your name's) route. Once you start adding employees you can categorize the clients on their route by the walkers name (example: Jessica's Dogs). Why is this important? Many of the messages you send out will only affect one or a few of the routes in your company but not the rest. With email programs you can choose to only email the contacts categorized "Jessica's Dogs" etc.

- Tag your emails so you can easily find them later. Over years your email folder can accumulate tens of thousands of emails. Tagging emails with keywords like "billing dispute," "referral opportunity," "difficult client," etc. helps you quickly sort though all of those old emails. It allows you to do your own data charts based on your tag searches.

Unique email addresses

Whether using Gmail or another email program, set up multiple email addresses to deal with the following:

- The contact email address on your website that will be used by prospective clients and all inquiries in general (example: *info@yourwebsite.com*).

- An email address just for existing clients (example: *clients@yourwebsite.com*).

- An email address for copies of all your bills to be sent (example: *bills@yourwebsite.com*). This comes in handy if you need to look up an old bill. All you'll have to do is search within the emails of this folder and you'll find your receipt.

- You'll want an email address for your existing walkers when you have some. (example: *walkers@yourwebsite.com*).

- This might be in the future but you should have an email address for prospective walkers (example: *newwalkers@yourwebsite.com*).

- You'll want to dedicate an email address for downloading software, registering on websites, etc. You never know which of these sites might sell your email address so you don't want them to have one you use with clients or anything important (example: *downloads@yourwebsite.com*).

- At some point you will have the need for a web designer, photographer, graphic designer, etc. (example: *design@yourwebsite.com*).

The point here is for you to have dedicated email addresses for all of these key areas of your business. If you group all of these areas into one mailbox you will inevitably be overrun with too many messages.

Group email tip

Make sure when you send a group email to clients to always do two things. First of all start the email by saying "this is a group email." If not you'll have a bunch of clients who think it's just meant for them and if they're on vacation they'll think you're crazy for not remembering and so on. Secondly make sure to add the clients' email addresses to the BCC: option in the email. BCC stands for "Blind Carbon Copy" and what it does is hide the clients' email addresses in the email. Clients appreciate this because some will not like you sending their private email to perfect strangers. And for your own benefit you don't want to get a few trouble making clients talking to each other.

Email to text (sent from your computer to a cell phone)

Once you have employees working for you, you might want to utilize the ability to email to text. Why? Imagine if you have to send and receive 100-200 messages a day and imagine if all of those messages are written on your cell phone? Modern day cell phone keyboards are comfortable but not as comfortable as the keyboard of a computer. Email to text also allows you to keep copies of your conversations on your computer. Also email to text is useful with your clients for reminders. Many clients are more likely to view a text message than an email. How do you email to text? You take the cell phone number you are emailing and then add the unique cell phone carrier code at the end.

Examples:

T-Mobile: CellPhoneNumber@tmomail.net
Verizon: CellPhoneNumber@vtext.com
AT&T: CellPhoneNumber@txt.att.net

The cell phone carrier codes might change over time so do a Google search on "email to sms carrier codes" to get the most up to date ones.

Email etiquette

I'm amazed at how curt/rude many people are when emailing or texting. This is an extremely bad trait to have considering how much people text and email for business these days. Some keys to email etiquette:

- *Greeting*: Say hello to the person you're contacting.
- *Upbeat*: Be positive, friendly and optimistic.
- *Be clear*: Email is ripe for misunderstandings. Save important or sensitive conversations for a phone call. Make your emails so clear that a six year old could understand them.

- *Full sentences*: Save your half-written and misspelled sentences for texting with your friends. But when you email or text a client, speak like you actually know the English language and not like you're a teenager.

- *Apologize*: Apologize if a mistake was made. Apologizing is an easy thing to do and it can make clients very happy. Don't let misunderstandings fester in a client's mind and turn into something much bigger than it actually is.

- *Use signatures at the end*: Create email signatures to end your message and have your name, phone number, website, email, etc.

Calendar events – reminders

Setting up reminders for yourself or employees for events outside of your normal schedule is extremely important! Luckily there are endless software's to help you do this.

Calendar events (on your computer)

Google Calendar is a free and user-friendly calendar software. It gives you an easy way to centralize all your important events and has great features like:

- Receive reminders to your cell phone or email.
- Share your schedule with clients and employees.
- Mobile version of Google Calendar on your cell phone (keeps your desktop and cell phone calendar in sync).
- Send invitations to events and track the answers of those you sent it to.
- Sync with desktop applications like Outlook, Apple iCal and Mozilla Sunbird.
- Work offline on your desktop.
- It conveniently syncs with Gmail and your cell phone.

On a Mac: Mac's iCal is a very powerful calendar and is great for setting up text message reminders for events.

Google Calendar's mobile version for your cell phone or your cell phone's own calendar is extremely useful. While you are running around all day it can be hard to remember events at the same time. Setting up calendar reminders on your cell phone the moment you learn of them is a great way to never forget an event again!

Open Office (text documents and spreadsheets)

For those of you who don't have a professional word processing or data entry program on your computer I highly suggest Google's Google Docs (online version) and the desktop version "Open Office" (PC version: *www.openoffice.org* / MAC version: *www.porting.openoffice.org/mac*). I would mainly use the Open Office software on your computer but the great thing about the online Google Docs is that it's like your own free network to share information. I have my employees update their notes on the animals they service on a monthly basis and they are able to do it online and I can access it immediately. If a walker gets sick and I need someone else to cover a route I just email the backup walker the online Google Doc and they can print out the dog notes from home.

Open Office word processing

For someone who doesn't already own Microsoft Word this is a great, free software package to use. The Open Office word processing functions like you'd expect any modern processing software to and has all the modern import and export options too. For whatever word processing software you'll be using you'll want to prepare the following documents:

- *Client application*: This is where the clients tell you about their dogs' quirks, health issues, etc. It's also where you get all the clients' contact information, vet information, building contacts, emergency contact, etc.

- *Permission to enter the apartment*: This letters states that you are allowed to be in a client's apartment and it will protect you if someone in the building ever questions you. Your clients must sign this letter.

- *Take to the vet in an emergency*: This letter states that you have the power to take a client's dog to a vet in the event of an emergency and the client can't be reached. If you don't have this letter a vet office might refuse to service a dog, even if it's an emergency! You need the clients to sign this letter.

- *Sign-in books*: Each client should have a sign-in book and in the sign-in book you chart your daily progress with your dogs. You can chart how long you walked, the dog's bathroom habits, energy level, if you found a mess when arriving, etc.

Sample forms: You can view examples of our forms here:
Log on to www.petsitterbible.com > *click the "pet service forms" tab*

Number crunching

For those of you who don't have Microsoft Excel, or another data entry program, Google Docs is a free program you can use to track numbers. If you're not familiar with how to use these programs click the help link, within *Google Docs,* and view the tutorials they offer. Spreadsheets in programs such as these can be a powerful tool in tracking your bills, creating a budget and many other items.

Keeping track of tax deductibles

Tax deductibles are items you've purchased for your company that can be deducted from your overall tax burden at the end of the year. I love tax deductions to be honest. I love the idea that investing in my company to try and grow it and create new jobs is rewarded. I find it to be very American actually. How do you keep track of your deductible purchases?

- As we discussed earlier you should dedicate an existing or new credit card to all of the purchases for your company.

- You should also set up a single bank account for company only purchases.

- You can use Excel if it's on your computer already or Google Office to track your deductibles.

- You should take 7-10 envelopes, mark what deductible category they cover and put all of your receipts into them based on category.

- You should consider purchasing Quicken software to track your expenses.

Quicken syncs with your online banking and credit card account. On a weekly basis you can download all of your purchases for that week and choose the deductible category they fall under. You can all memorize companies you buy items from a lot (for me that would be Staples) and then every time Quicken downloads a charge from Quicken it will automatically apply the deductible category you told it to.

Learn more here: www.quicken.intuit.com

Note: When it comes to preparing your personal income taxes I would not recommend using tax software like Turbo Tax. I would highly recommend you use a personal accountant instead. The personal service you receive from a good accountant can't be matched.

Billing

Before you start walking a client's dog, set up the accounting and payment schedule! Early on with my business, I took checks and cash. I also consistently had clients running balances of multiple weeks. I was naïve then and never worried much about not being paid at the end of the day. I mean, we were taking care of their dogs, right? Early on I let clients run up very large balances with me and it greatly hampered my ability to grow. Think about it, if you continue to pay your walkers weekly (even if you're not paid) that's money you could be using to grow your company. What I learned was that I would never again give the clients the power to decide when and how they would pay me. From that point on, I went strictly to credit cards on file and never let clients get more than two weeks behind. I recommend you do the same. It's extremely cumbersome to grow your business while being paid by check and cash. In that scenario, you need to depend on the client to leave the payment on a weekly basis, the walker to pick it up and then of course you need to prepare everything before going to wait in line at the bank. And that gets exhausting very quickly!

On the flip side when you accept credit cards you do have to pay a processing fee for receiving the cards. But it is a proven fact that customers will spend more money with credit cards and I highly recommend receiving payment through credit cards.

Tip: Do not let your clients get behind on paying their bills. Make it clearly known on your invoices that bills need to be paid within a few days of the invoice date. Maybe have a company policy that you halt service if a client gets more than two weeks behind on bills. Trust me on this, there are some clients who would go without paying you for a year straight

if you let them. Since creating my company policy of not allowing clients to get behind on their bills my life has become much easier.

Tip: You can investigate this further through an accountant but I would strongly suggest you confirm if you need to charge sales tax in your state. If it turns out you do need to collect sales tax you can ask your accountant where you need to sign up for this. And if you do start collecting sales tax you should put this money aside every week and make sure not to spend it, because it's not your money to spend. You'll need to set up reminders for yourself of the dates to pay your sales tax through the year. If you don't pay sales tax on time you will be penalized.

Tip: Put money aside every week, even if it's $5 and make this a trend. One of the main reasons you're doing all this is to make money and don't loose track of that. Start putting money away from the very beginning, even if it's only symbolic.

Bill keeping software programs and methods

In the beginning you have a few things to consider when it comes to billing your clients:

- *Creating invoices*: Clients appreciate receiving a weekly invoice. It looks and feels professional. Even if they don't look at it, they just like knowing it's there.

- *Delivering invoices:* Delivering invoices electronically through email as a pdf file is much easier for you than dropping them off at clients' homes and looks professional to your clients.

- *Being paid:* Your choice is cash *and* check *or* credit cards. I would not offer both and ideally I would only accept credit cards if I were you. Again this looks professional but it's also a proven fact that people spend more on credit cards than they ever would writing out a check or taking cash out of an ATM every week. There are costs involved with receiving credit cards, but I think they are outweighed by the increase in spending you'll receive. One note on credit cards: I would try and avoid accepting American Express, Rewards and or Corporate Cards. Cards such as these cost you a higher fee to process. Don't get me wrong, checks and cash are great too but there are problems involved with accepting them. It requires your clients to remember to pay you on time and that will not be as easy as paying with a credit card. And once you receive the payments you then need to manually chart each payment, make sure nothing is missing and then deposit it into the bank.

Here are a few different ways you could handle your billing:

- Google Docs/Open Office Suite (free):
- Excel / Word (depends if they are pre-installed):
- Quickbooks simple start (free with confitions):
- Quickbooks desktop or online (paid):
- Paypal invoice maker (free to send):
- Google checkout (free to send):

Programs to prepare and track your weekly and yearly numbers

Google Docs/Open Office Suite (free)

In these programs you can chart your weekly numbers and even keep a running tally for the year and run reports. Take the time to master these programs if you don't know them already. You can find endless tutorials through the help section and ask questions in the community section too. If you're not accepting invoices through credit card you can create invoices with Google Docs word processing program.

Excel/Word (free if pre-installed in your computer)

You can accomplish the same things here as in Google Docs and Open Office Suite. The one difference is that Google Docs is online and offers the benefit of being web accessible.

Want to avoid any processing fees? Then accept checks and cash as your form of payment at least in the beginning. But I honestly don't think you can build a large, professional company and not take credit cards at some point.

Programs to prepare and track your weekly numbers PLUS receive payments

Quickbooks Simple Start (free with conditions):
(www.quickbooks.intuit.com)

I'm a huge fan of Quickbooks and Quickbooks Simple Start is a great place to get familiar with the software if you've never used it before. The software is free to get started but once you get above 5 clients you'd need to upgrade to a version that carries a low monthly fee.

Quickbooks desktop or online:
(www.quickbooks.intuit.com)

Quickbooks is the king of small business accounting software programs. In this powerful software you can consolidate in one place all of your billing, payments to vendors, payroll reporting and even do direct deposits to your future employees. Quickbooks offers both a desktop version and an online version. In both software applications you have the ability to either prepare invoices and have your clients pay them or to keep credit cards on file and charge the cards yourself. You'll need to set up a merchant account to receive credit card payment but Quickbooks can walk you through the process within the software and they make it very easy. The merchant rates you'll be charged to accept credit cards might be a little higher than using PayPal or Google Checkout but the ease of use and consolidation and sorting ability of Quickbooks might make it worthwhile for you.

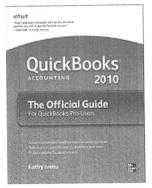

If you decide to use Quickbooks I'd try and learn as much as you can to fully utilize all its power. There are plenty of tutorials within the software and on Quickbooks' site too: *(www.support.quickbooks.intuit.com/support/)*. But at some point you might want to consider purchasing Quickbooks' own guide books (the 2010 addition is pictured).

Programs to receive payments from your clients

PayPal Invoices: (www.merchant.paypal.com)

Paypal Merchant Services offers a user friendly platform to collect payments from your clients. Within PayPal you can create invoices for your clients and clients have numerous ways to pay their bills. They pay through email, through their cell phones or on your website. Once your clients pay their bills the money can go directly into the bank account you specify. There is a small fee applied per transaction and it does seem to be a little more expensive than Google Checkout. At the moment PayPal does seem to provide more convenient ways for your clients to pay you. You can view a running tally of what clients have paid, what clients haven't, etc.

Google Checkout: (https://checkout.google.com)

Google Checkout allows you to prepare and email your clients' invoices. When the clients open the invoice they can immediately pay you through credit card. You are charged a small fee to receive money (as low as 1.9%) but there are no additional fees as of today at least. The money you receive is deposited straight into your bank account.

Cell Phones

Cell phones are getting to the point where they are going to replace the need for laptops. Cell phones and specifically "smart phones" allow you to be out and about but still have all the powers of your office. A good "smart phone" can receive emails, type emails, open word documents and spreadsheets as well as edit these documents. Prospective clients for my company are routinely amazed at how fast I get back to them and it's because of my "smart phone." If a new client emails me or submits a new customer request form I receive it within a minute or two and I will immediately call them. Your smart phone can also sync up to your computer and take with it all your company contacts and your Calendar events (Google

Calendar, iCal, etc.). If you add new information to your "smart phone" while out and about you can sync your phone back to your computer later that day and add the new information to your desktop. The seamless ability to have access to all your company information, in your office or out, is extremely powerful. It gives you freedom!

Cell phone camera and video camcorder

Think of the benefit of a "smart phone" that can also shoot nice pictures and videos! You can email photos to your clients of their dogs on a walk or happy at home in real time through your "smart phone." Clients love small touches like this. It makes them feel like they are actually there with you as you perform the job and they see their dog is happy and safe.

Upgrading your cell phone and plan

There are a few things you need to consider if you don't presently have a smart phone and want to get one:

- *Upgrade*: Do you qualify for an upgrade with your cell phone carrier?

- *Data plan*: Outside of the phone what is your data plan? If you plan to send lots of images and maybe even videos you should verify what type of plan you have and roughly how many images you'll be able to send with it. Going over your data allowance on a cell phone can be costly.

- *Cell phone carrier*: Do you like your present cell phone carrier? If you don't and you only have a few months before your contract runs out you might want to wait it out and then go to another provider when the contract does run out. As a new customer with another carrier you'll get a great deal on a "smart phone."

- *Sell your contract/avoid cancellation fee*: Do you have a long time left on your cell phone contract and you don't like your carrier? Try this website to learn more: *www.cellswapper.com.*

- *Texting*: Texting is very popular these days and you might want to go with an unlimited texting plan if you find yourself routinely getting close to going over your limit. Your positive and active interaction with the clients will increase profits and keep clients in the company. Being able to contact your clients as much as you or they want is very important and don't let the $10-$20 month of a cell phone plan stop that. It will be money well spent.

- *Insurance*: In a business such as this where you will be running around in all types of weather I'd recommend getting insurance on your phone. For a small monthly fee you can get a replacement phone for a low price or free depending on the circumstances of what happens to your phone.

- *Battery life*: The battery life of your phone is very important. You'll need a phone that has a strong battery life. The last thing you want to do is be charging your phone while running around or even worse lose all power to your phone all together.

To view cell phone reviews I would suggest going to (*www.cnet.com/*) and clicking "cell' and on that page click "best smart phones."

Estimated increase to cell phone bill: (-$30 a month)
Money Remaining: ($218)

Cell Phone Quick Notes

Here are some quick notes you might want to consider when it comes to cell phones:

- *The Android operating system*: This is Google's cell phone operating system. Get ready to find it offered in lots of new cell phones. It's an extremely user friendly operating system and it seamlessly combines touch screen and physical keyboards on *the same phone*! This is really the best of both worlds. Also if you wind up using a lot of the free Google apps we have discussed (Gmail, Google Calendar, Google Docs, Picasa Image, You Tube, etc.) you will find especially easy integration with *Android phones*.

- *Touch screen vs. physical keypads*: Personally I could never use a touch screen keyboard to type as many message as I do a day. No matter how touch sensitive they make a touch screen it will never match a physical keyboard in my mind. For someone on the move like you will be in this business I would highly recommend having a physical keyboard on your phone.

- *Blackberry*: Blackberrys make excellent business phones, maybe the best phones for business and messaging. Blackberry has listened to the cries for more social features and they have added better digital cameras, video cameras and sync abilities for music too. I've used many Blackberrys and highly recommend them for this type of business.

- *Backup your data*: All smart phones have desktop software you can use to backup your cell phone data on your computer. If you don't have or can't find the software that came with the cell phone try going on the manufacturer's website and downloading it from there. Try and backup your cell phone's information once a week or at the least once a month.

- *Sync with your computer*: On a weekly basis the information on your computer will change and the information on your cell phone will change too. To keep both of them up to date you should actively sync your cell phone with your computer.

- *Tips and tricks*: Take the time to learn all the tips and tricks of your phone. It's rare these days that a smart phone doesn't have many user-friendly options to make your life easier. Take the time to read the user manual that comes with the phone. But maybe also search out user groups/discussion boards on the Internet for users of your phone. There are tons of small tricks you can do to save time on your cell phone and stay more organized (example: if you find a cell phone number or email address in an email you can put your cursor over it and it should highlight the number or email address – there should then be an option to immediately add that information to an existing contact on your phone or create a brand new one from the information – this is a great way to keep track of information and not repeatedly have to ask someone for their contact information.)

- *Side note*: Smart Phones are great but they are addictive. When you go out to dinner or come home I'd recommend putting your phone away, turning off the ringer, etc. It's rare you will get a message worth angering your loved ones or making you anxious from checking your phone so often.

Estimate cell phone case: (-$30)
Money remaining: ($188)

Project management software

If you're like me you probably have multiple projects running at all times and it can be hard to keep track of all of them. I started using a software recently that I have found invaluable to manage multiple projects at one time and it's called Basecamp. Here's the link to check it out: *www.basecamphq.com/signup*

They offer a free version you can try out to see how you like it.

Note: I also like to use marker boards to chart my ideas for the day, week, month, year, etc. You can purchase marker boards of all sizes at competitive prices from Staples (*www.staples.com/*)

Love your work area

Your work area should be a place you love visiting. I love the work area I've built in my house and I've clearly seen the positive impact that has had on my work. My work area used to be chaotic and my work reflected that. The following are some of the things I want you to consider with your computer and your work area:

- *Chair:* A comfortable ergonomic computer chair that supports your back will make you very happy!

- *Ergonomic:* Ergonomic wrist rests in front of your keyboard (for desktops) and for your mouse.

- *Monitor height:* The height of your monitor should be accurate or you can more easily strain your back and eyes. Learn more: *www.office-ergo.com/setting.htm.*

- *Work area:* Try and position your work area near a window where you can feel a nice breeze when you want or get some extra light in the room. But if you do position your work area near a window make sure you don't put your computer or any other electronic appliances too close to an open window, in case it rains.

- *Monitor:* Are you using an old monitor? Older monitors have mercury in them and can both hurt your eyes and be unhealthy for you over time. If you're looking to upgrade to a new monitor I highly recommend you buy a wide screen LCD monitor that doesn't contain mercury and also uses a fraction of the energy of older monitors. If you'll need to use an old monitor for awhile longer I'd consider buying an anti-glare screen that will both lessen the glare on your eyes and also protect you from radiation in the monitor.

- *Anti-glare/glossy screens*: Does your monitor have anti-glare in it? Is it glossy? Glossy screens and screens that don't have anti-glare can cause you major eyestrain. If your current monitor causes you eyestrain but you can't presently purchase a new one there are still options. You can purchase an anti-glare screen or film online from companies like 3M. If you do purchase a new screen try and buy one that is not glossy and has anti-glare built into it. Especially try to buy a monitor that does not have any mercury in it.

- *Aesthetic of work area*: Put some nice pictures or artwork that you love in your work area. I wouldn't put anything too intense. Try to make your work area calming and inviting. Maybe paint your work area a nice calm color and add some plants. Whatever it is that will relax you but also not distract you would be a good idea.

- *Organize work area*: You want to have your work area well organized. Your printer should be positioned close to your desk so you don't even need to stand up to grab printed materials. You should try and have a desk with storage built right in and if you don't, a filing cabinet might be a great idea. Stores like "The Container Store" and "Staples" offer great filing and organization materials.

Your office starts with your computer

In this digital age your computer might have the single biggest impact on your company, with your cell phone being a close second. I'm not saying they are more important than you, your message or your dedication. But your computer and your cell phone are largely what will connect you with your potential clients. Your computer and your cell phone allow you to broadcast your message so thousands of people can learn what a great company you've built. Without being digitally connected you will be waiting and hoping some-one will knock on your door for business.

You need to be prepared by doing the following:

- *Update software*: There are mixed beliefs about how often you should update your computer's software. Some believe it's best to be a little bit behind so you don't have to deal with the new bugs software will have. Others believe you should update your software religiously the moment an update is available. But whatever you believe if you haven't updated your computer's software for months, or even years, I would recommend doing so now!

- *Age of computer*: A computer can become old very quickly these days, within 2-3 years of purchase in fact. Upgrading your browser (Windows 7, Mac OSX, etc.) as new ones come out will help keep your computer "younger." But there are just so many ways you can upgrade your computer to stay with the times. And if your computer is 3-4 years old you might want to consider purchasing a new one or at the least updating your current computer.

- *Key areas within a computer*: There are three main areas within a computer that contribute to its performance and they are: *processor speed, hard drive size* and *total ram*. You can easily upgrade your hard drive and ram over time but it's a little more detailed to upgrade your processor and it's *not* possible to upgrade your processor in a laptop. So with that said if you are purchasing a new computer and can only afford one upgrade to the computer I'd spend that money on upgrading the processor speed. If you have an existing computer and want to upgrade the ram crucial.com (*www.crucial.com/*) is a good place to find ram for PC's and Apple.com (*www.store.apple.com/us*) is the place for Macs.

- *PC vs. Mac:* There are believed to be two types of computer users, PC users and Mac users. Personally I use both Mac and PC. I use a Mac for almost every aspect of my business except for my accounting. I use a PC for accounting because the software I use (Quickbooks) is not yet as good in the Mac version. Would I switch completely to Mac when and if Quickbooks catches up in the Mac version? Absolutely. "Why?" you might ask? Personally I find the overall experience on a Mac to be more pleasant and relaxing. I find PCs often have issues and of course they are exposed to many viruses while Macs are not. A Mac can be hacked just like a PC but the chances of a Mac getting a crippling virus are slim to none. If you can afford a Mac and plan to use a different accounting program than mine, or an online accounting software I'd highly recommend a Mac. Speaking of price, Macs do cost more but based on the quality of the product, I feel it's more than worth it.

- *Used computers*: Should you buy a used computer? Personally I wouldn't buy a used computer or used electronics in general. I think the used computer market is so shady and unless you know the person you're buying from personally I wouldn't trust it. If you happen to buy a used computer from a stranger I would recommend replacing the hard drive at least.

Protecting your clients personal information

I am extra sensitive when it comes to protecting my clients' personal information. Compromising your clients' personal information can create a bad buzz about your company and lead to lost clients very quickly. I find the following items to be essential in protecting your clients' information:

- *Paper shredder*: Shred everything and anything to do with you or your clients' personal information and only use a "cross-cut paper shredder."

- *External firewall*: An external firewall is necessary as opposed to an internal firewall. It actually keeps people out of your computer.

- *Anti-virus and spyware software*: Norton routinely receives high praise for products of this type.

- *Encrypt sensitive data*: Softwares like WinZip can encrypt sensitive data both on your computer and on external drives.

- *Safe email*: You should ask your clients *never* to email you a new credit card number. Unfortunately, emails are routinely caught by hackers.

- *Strangers*: Do not give out keys or any type of personal information to someone you do not recognize as the owner.

Norton Anti-Virus: (-$70)
*Money remaining: **($118)***

With your remaining budget: Maybe it's time to buy some more business cards? Or some more images from istockphoto.com for your website? Or instead maybe your remaining money could be the down payment on a digital camera? Or for next month's Ad Word's bill?

If you have more money to spend

At this point if you can spend more on your business that's great, but no matter what, you have created an excellent foundation to your company. Here is a list of ideas and products for you to think about for now or in the future:

- *External hard drive:* An external hard is a very simple and effective way to backup you computer's information. Just imagine if your computer died today. What would you do? If you had an external hard drive you'd be okay. Try and purchase an external hard drive that is encrypted for safety.

- *Web designer:* The importance of having a quality website can't be overstated. Look hard to find a great web designer you can afford. All of the investments I've made in my websites have paid for themselves ten times over.

- *Graphic designer:* A good graphic designer is invaluable when it comes to your website. If you find someone whose work you love and can afford, keep them happy and do lots of projects with them over time.

- *Quickbooks Pro or Premiere:* Quickbooks Pro or Premiere will allow you to centralize your billing, payroll and much more. Quickbooks not only helps you collect your weekly billing, it also helps you understand how you make your money and where you should maybe put more emphasis.

- *Digital camera:* Your clients love images of their dogs and so will visitors to your website. I would highly recommend investing in a pocket size digital camera when you're able to. I've personally had great luck with Canon digital cameras. You can research camera reviews at *www.cnet.com.*

- *HD camcorder or Flip:* Video is the way of the future and you can stay ahead of the trends by offering lots of video clips of your dogs and walkers. If you can't presently afford an HD camcorder go with The Flip pocket camcorder.

End of chapter checklist

- Update your software and Browsers.

- Create a Google Account and look into their free email, accounting and word processing programs.

- Master all the features of your email program.

- Start using a calendar program that offers email and text reminders.

- Choose a software to track billing and create invoices.

- Decide if you want to be paid by credit card or check and cash.
- Optimize your phone or upgrade to a smart phone.
- Try and have a cell phone that can take good pictures, is easy to type on and has a large memory.
- Make sure you are with the best possible cell carrier for your area.
- Sync your cell phone with your computer and vice versa.
- Optimize or upgrade your computer.
- Create a comfortable and organized space to in which to work.
- Purchase ergonomic products to protect yourself against injury.
- Protect and guard your clients' personal information.

Chapter 8

Dealing with New Clients, Setting Up Routes, Pet Sits

Clients

You might not realize it but you probably already have a very strong skill set to deal with clients. Have you ever done sales? Have you ever dealt with customers on the phone or in person? Have you ever been an assistant to someone? Have you ever had to tend to someone's requests? Most likely I'll assume you said yes to a few of these and your past experiences will come in very handy.

I love my clients and the experience I've had with my clients. Doing this job has put me into the homes of very powerful and interesting people and I've learned a lot from them. In my experiences with my clients I have created friends and mentors and learned a lot from them. Don't get me wrong, dealing with the demands of my clients is not easy but doing a good job of it can be very rewarding both on a personal and business level.

Your rates

The amount you charge for your service will be directly associated with your success and happiness. Here are some tips on deciding what to charge:

- *Study the market*: Who are your competitors in the market? By competitors I mean companies that offer similar types of services. Study the price points for the lowest and highest prices being offered in your area. What separates the two? And how does your service compare? If you're just starting your company, then base this decision on what you see your company becoming.

- *How will you set yourself apart from the competition*: Will you offer an exceedingly high level of customer service and a high price point? Will you offer casino style customer service where all the needs of your clients are taken care of the drop of a dime? Or will you be the Walmart of your area, offering the lowest price point with limited customer service?

- *How much will pay your walkers*: Even if you are presently an individual dog walker you want to keep in mind how much you will pay your employees in the future. Your price point needs to be high enough to pay your walkers a living wage while also providing yourself enough income.

- *What will you classify your walkers as:* This will be discussed more in the employees section but there's a big financial difference between classifying your walkers as independent contractors vs. employees. If you classify your walkers as employees it will increase your costs anywhere from 10-15% a year. You'll need to keep this in mind when deciding your prices.

- *Weekly rates:* For pet services like dog walking, dog running and walk and trains you'll service your clients on a daily/weekly basis. It's important that you get the most out of each spot on a route to ensure you and your walkers make enough money. A typical dog walking client will want service Monday-Friday. If a client wants less than 5 days a week you should consider having them pay more per walk. It's a custom practice for our industry and helps lessen the blow when clients are off.

- *Cancellation fees*: Cancellation fees are also normal for our business because short-notice cancellation can cause havoc on your routes. If a client cancels within 24 hr's you should consider charging a cancellation fee.

- *Non-negotiable rates*: Outside of a handful of cases I have never negotiated my rates with my clients. I feel it's important that you stand strong on your rates. If you give an inch on negotiating your rates some clients will take a yard and it will never stop. I also don't like the idea of different clients having different rates. The only time I think this is okay is when you want to raise rates on incoming clients. If it's not a good time to raise rates on existing clients but it is on incoming clients, I think that's fine.

What I did: I studied the market in New York City and have tried to make sure I've never been the cheapest nor the most expensive. I do believe that Downtown Pets offers a high level of professionalism and customer service that few other services in the area provide. Over time as I've found my niche I've tried to compare my company to other companies of similar services and values. In the end I charge what is necessary to provide myself, and my walkers a living wage.

The following are my present rates and how I charge based on the total walks per week:

Rate List

Service (quantity in a week):	Per walk:
15 min walk (5+)	$12
15 min walk (4)	$13.25
15 min walk (3)	$14
15 min walk (2)	$14
15 min walk (1)	$15
30 min walk (5+)	$17
30 min walk (4)	$18.25
30 min walk (3)	$19
30 min walk (2)	$19
30 min walk (1)	$20
50 min walk	$24
45 min dog runner	$40
30 min dog runner	$30

20 min dog runner $20

- For holidays, weekends, nights (past 6pm), Morning's (before 9am) and 2nd dog please add ($7).
- Sleepovers are ($80) for the first dog and ($35) for each additional dog and include a morning and evening walk.
- There is a 24 hr policy on cancellations and the cancellation fee is ($10.66).
- For short-term / sporadic clients add ($7) per walk.
- If you come off the route for more than 3 weeks there is a 30% (of a normal week) weekly fee to hold your spot on the route.

Some things to notice about my rate sheet

- *Diversity of services:* You'll notice we offer dog walking, pet sitting and dog running. I point this out because I want to stress how you can expand your services over time. When we first started we only offered dog walking and pet sitting. We only expanded into dog running once we had created structure for it. I'd recommend you start with one or two main services and master them before expanding. In the near future we plan to start offering our own in-house dog training and we have been preparing for this service over a year.

- *Early, late, holiday, weekend etc.:* I think it's important to pay your walkers extra when they are working at inconvenient times. There's not a huge demand for nights, weekends, holidays or weekends. Paying your walkers extra to do these walks will keep their interest in doing them.

- *Short-term / sporadic:* Walk and train, dog walking and dog running businesses usually prefer regular Monday-Friday clients. Short-term and sporadic clients are great ways for you to fill gaps in your routes and to make some extra money. If you do offer this service I'd recommend charging more than your usual rates. Keep in mind that you are assuming liability for the owner's home and pet. That's a big burden to take on for a short-term client and it's why you should make more if you decide to take them on.

- *Holding Fee:* Clients will come off the routes for all sorts of reasons (leaving their job, on vacation, injured). I've learned over time that some clients who say they'll be back on the route in 5 weeks never come back at all! So I'd suggest you have some type of holding fee. If your client is off for more than 3 weeks they need to pay a holding fee to hold their spot on the route. For those clients who don't understand why this is necessary explain to them that you are losing money while they are off and you will turn away new business to reserve their spot.

Raising Prices

You should raise your prices over time. It's necessary to be able to compete, grow and increase payroll, among other things. All businesses raise prices to compete in changing markets but a lot of pet services seem slow to do so. I think the reason is because so many people in the pet service industry do not have a business background. There is a benefit to having competitors raise their prices because it raises prices for the entire market. If you run into a competitor charging drastically less than market rates try and give them a gentle recommendation of for raising rates. The point is though don't be scared to do gradual increases rates over time. The increased income you'll receive will do wonders for your company and clients expect to have rates go up over time.

What I did

I've raised rates twice over the past 6 years with each increase being $1. One dollar doesn't seem like much but when you apply it to the number of dogs we have and the amount of walks we do it's actually a lot of money. The key is to make sure your starting price point is profitable so you don't have to drastically raise rates on *** short notice, which could bother some clients.

Some clients will get angry when you raise prices

There will always be clients who get angry when you raise prices. Some people simply don't understand the concept of raising prices and how it's necessary in most businesses. While still other clients will not understand why a dog walking company will need to raise prices. Explain your reasons to clients like these, make a few deals here or there but you have nothing to apologize for. If you go to the same newsstand over 5 years the price for a Gatorade will probably go up 2 times over that period. Raising prices is a part of doing business and an easy way to add a cash influx to your company and stay competitive.

First Contact with Potential Clients

They say you only get one chance to make a first impression and it's true. Whether on the phone or in an email you want to immediately set a tone with your prospective clients. You want to be friendly, confident and show a true interest in their pets' needs. I've listed some keys to dealing with new clients below:

- *Smile as you answer the phone:* Each time you go to answer your phone for a potential new client smile as you pick up the phone. Why? Because you will sound like you are smiling, happy and welcoming even if you're in a terrible mood. A simple smile on your face can brighten the sound of your voice.

- *Make it personal as quickly as possible:* No matter what questions your prospective client starts out with, make sure to make the conversation personal as quickly as you can. How can you make the conversation personal? Just think about it. The person on the other end of the line is trying to find someone to come into their homes while they are not there and to take care of their pets, often considered more like members of the family. So what should you talk about? Talk about their dogs as quickly as you can. Try and find out the pet's name and from that point on in the conversation use the pet's name whenever mentioning them. Find out what breed the pet is. If you've encountered that breed before or the issues they describe their pet having, try and share your own experience. Be brief when it comes to your own experience, you're really here to listen to them but personalizing the conversation as quickly as possible is very powerful. A potential client might call you up and immediately start asking you about your prices or ask for references but the moment you get them talking about their pets on a personal level you'll see a whole different side of your clients. They will relax and for a brief moment in their busy day you'll just be talking about one of the most enjoyable things in their lives, their pets.

- *Know your stuff:* One of the best decisions I made with my business was to educate myself as much as possible on the keys areas of the pet service industry. I've tried to learn as much as possible about tending to a pet's health, safety and happiness. Being able to display this knowledge over the phone can very quickly put a prospective client at ease. If your prospective client just got a new puppy and doesn't know the first thing about raising a puppy you will really impress them by being able to talk about your philosophies on house training, leash training and puppy proofing a house. Not only will this strong knowledge of animals help you get more clients, it will also help you maximize the business you get from your clients but we'll discuss that more later in the chapter.

- *Provide solutions to your clients' problems:* This is what you're here to do but it's also a great way to increase profit in your company. You are here to provide solutions for your clients and their pets' problems and that's really what makes you a professional pet service. If you are not able to possess or develop an advanced knowledge of pets then what's the difference between you and the neighbor's kid? If you just take the dog out to go to the bathroom and don't provide much more, it's hard to say you're a professional dog walker. We've already discussed this, but you'll want to be well educated on at least the following:
  1. Safety Guidelines
  2. House training
  3. Leash training
  4. Equipment
  5. How a client's house is setup

6.   Aggression

7.   Separation anxiety.

- *Listen:* It sounds easy enough, right? But our generation seems to have a problem with listening. We always want the chance to express our opinion and too often lose the opportunity to learn just by keeping our mouths closed and listening. Your best opportunity to learn about your prospective clients might be during your first conversation and or the first week or two in contact. Listen closely to your clients. Do you offer what this client is looking for? If not do you want to offer it? Think hard before you commit to a service that pushes you outside of your comfort zone.

Example: A client wants night walks, between 9pm-10pm seven days a week. Sounds like a lot of work and a lot of money, right? But assuming they don't live near you, do you want to be coming home at 11pm every night for a few extra dollars a day? That's for you to decide, I just want to make sure you listen closely to what your clients are looking for and make sure it fits your business plan. Are they looking for short-term or sporadic service? Do they live in your area or much farther away?

- *Take notes:* What are they looking for? Concerns? Bad experiences they had with past places? When do they want to start (set a reminder to follow- up). If they say they are still calling a few places ask if you could at least email them some information. The more you know about how they are taking care of their dogs the more advice you can offer and problems you can help solve. Your clients' problems require your solutions.

How do you qualify a client?

How do you qualify a client to make sure they are right for you? You need to base this on your business plan and find out the following too:

- *Area*: Are they located in your service area?

- *Aggression*: Ask specific questions about dog aggression before beginning service.

- *Out of area*: If they are not in your service area try and refer them to someone you've made a relationship with and make sure they tell that company you referred them.

- *Services*: Find out what they are looking for in terms of services, times of the day and consistency.

- *Not sure what they want*: At this point, you should have a fair idea if it sounds like a good fit. Be wary of a client who originally responds for services you do not offer but decides to go with you anyway. You still might want to give it a shot, wow them into loving you, but don't be surprised if they keep looking elsewhere for what they want while working with you.

- *Policies*: Make sure to tell them your prices and payment structure too. The last thing you want is for someone to come back to you two months from now, acting like they were tricked into something.

Common questions you might hear from prospective clients

- What are your prices?
- What are your service times?
- Is it individual walks or pack walks?
- What is the process to get started?
- How long have you been in business?
- Where areas do you service?
- What services do you offer?
- Do you offer any special services for dealing with puppies? With aggressive dogs?

- Are you bonded and insured? What does it even mean to be bonded and insured?

- Can you do weekends, nights, short-notice?

- What's your cancellation policy?

Practice having friends ask you these questions over the phone and work on your answers. Get your mojo going, get confident with your answers. If you have no clients make it seem like you have 30. If you have 30 make it seem like you have 50 and so on. You haven't been in business for three weeks you've been in business for 3 years. Now don't get me wrong, I'm not recommending you lie to your clients, I'm recommending you think this way. If you think it you will act it and your clients will pick up on it. Remember, act as if! Also remember that no matter how you start you'll get better at speaking on the phone.

Speaking to prospective clients

Below I've listed common interactions you'll have with prospective clients and some recommendations on how to deal with them.

Shoppers

Prospective Client

"Well I'm just trying to get a sense of the market and I'm calling a bunch of different places and-"

"Well thanks so much for the information, I'm just starting my search and-"

"Well I'm just preparing now, we're looking to start in a month or two-"

"Well thanks a lot, let me speak to my partner and-"

You

"I understand. Well I would like to just tell you a few ways we're different than most of the competition." –or– "I understand. Well, how about I grab your email address and send you some information about our company?" If you don't have some type of contact information you might never hear from this person again.

The point is to create a connection with this client both personally and digitally. If you're able to get an email address you will now have them on file and can email them a small packet about your company and in the near future you can write them a follow-up email. My follow-up emails have led to lots of business I never would have had if I hadn't taken email addresses over the phone.

Clients who show interest but no urgency

Prospective Client

"We're looking to start in the next few weeks and-"

"Well we could meet anytime over the next week or two-"

"I'm free tonight at 8pm but if that's too late I can do next week sometime-"

You

"Well you know, we can actually meet tonight if you're able to? If not, how about tomorrow night?"

The point is you've already an interest your company and you don't want to let that subside. Meet them in person as quickly as possible and try and get them into your company. If it's the difference between meeting them tonight at an off hour vs. next week I'd meet them at the off hour. Why risk the chance of having them sign with a competitor?

Clients who want to get started right away

I don't think you need any advice here, right? Meet them right away!

Clients who aren't a fit for your company (want different services than you offer, are out of your service area, etc.)

Prospective client

"I live outside of your service area-"

"I'm looking for a service you don't offer nor want to offer-"

You

"Well I have a great referral I could give you in your area and mentioning that I referred you will definitely help."

Bad signs in a client

They spend lots of time badmouthing past walkers. Find out exactly what problems they had with their past walkers and see if you think they are rational complaints. Or are you about to become the new dog walking company they will be badmouthing?

They badmouth their dogs

Sounds strange, right? But it happens. This might be someone you need to try and educate more about his or her own dog.

Loopy clients

They are all over the place in regards to what they're looking for, they are loopy etc. This is not always the mark of a bad client but you'll want to make a mental note that they are loopy. Over time this can be a trait to worry about.

Clients who ask endless questions before starting and want to talk to you for hours upon hours about the potential dog they are bringing home

Funny enough I have found that these types of clients will often not wind up going with your company and or staying. This is the sign of a shopper or an an overly neurotic client.

Meeting the clients and their pets

Here are some keys when meeting a prospective client in person:

- *Be presentable:* This doesn't mean you need to be wearing a suit. But if you normally wear a hat crooked to the side, etc. then straighten yourself out a bit before you meet the client. Just don't look like a mess or too shabby. Some clients will be scared off by this, although they will not verbalize that to you, they will silently judge you. Why lose a client because of how you are dressed? And it goes without saying you shouldn't wear any drug themed shirts and nothing too aggressive or threatening.

- *Be on time:* Dog walking is a job that involves keeping a schedule with the pets and if you don't show up on time for your initial meeting how can you be trusted to visit their pet on time? I would show up a few minutes early if possible to impress them. If you are running late give them notice and apologize for it.

- *Be cheerful:* Even if you are not in a good mood, be cheerful and try and smile as much as you can. The prospective client wants to trust and like you and they want to tell you about the pet they love so much sitting next to them. Nothing can bum a client out more than finding a depressed prospective sitter or walker sitting in front of them.

- *Concentrate on their pet:* Many of the clients want to see how you interact with their pet and how interested you are. About the worst thing you could do is not show an interest. Bring a treat for the pet with you, and try and make sure it's vegetarian or organic. Ask the client if it would be okay to give their pet a treat and then ask if it has any food allergies. The client will appreciate your concern for their pet's health and giving a pet a treat can be a nice icebreaker. From that point on try and concentrate on the pet but don't crowd it, don't pursue it, let it come to you.

- *Be honest:* What I mean by honest is to be up front about your policies and what you offer. If you love this prospective client but they are looking for services you just can't or don't want to offer you need to be honest about it. So if they are looking for short-notice late night walks (and this wasn't discussed in your initial phone conversation) and you just can't do it, you need to tell them. Remember you need to set boundaries with the clients because if not they will take as much as you'll give them.

- *If the meeting is going too long:* Sometimes in the midst of being interviewed by a prospective client you'll realize you've been there 20 minutes, even 30 minutes and that honestly is about as much time as a client should need when meeting you. Anything more might be reflective of a shopper or someone who is a bit neurotic. Either way if you feel the meeting has gone past a necessary time feel free to tell the client you don't mean to cut them off but you do have another appointment to get to. Some walkers think a 1-hour interview with a prospective client is a good sign but I don't. I feel this is usually the sign of a client who will not go with your company or if they do, they'll likely be a difficult client.

- *After meeting the clients:* If the clients don't give you a set of keys to their home at the end of the visit don't be disappointed. They might just need some time to mull over the decision. I would email them the next day to tell them you enjoyed meeting them and hope to work together. If you don't hear back from them for a few days I'd write one more email saying you were just checking in to see if they'd like to move forward with service.

Close them

While I don't feel you ever "sell" when it comes to the pet service industry, I do feel you "close." You're not pushing products and services here. You are listening to your clients' needs and trying to create the best possible solutions to help them. But at the same time you do need to get your prospective clients into the company and that might take some salesmanship. Outside of your prospective clients who just like to shop around, most clients want to be able to stop their search. They want to like you and you need to do your best to let them. I've discussed a few of the ways you can accomplish this above but now you need to have a system for going forward. "Okay so where do we go from here," the prospective client might say. You want to do the following:

- If you haven't already, immediately email them an application or if you haven't received one back yet make sure to request it.
- Create a user account in your email program for them: (dog name, email address, mobile number, address, vet, emergency contact, other person involved with dog contact).
- Sync contact information onto your cell phone.
- If you will not be the walker, give the walker a copy of the application.
- Put keys on a solid key chain with a tag on it (no addresses, just put the dog's name).
- Arrange for their payment information.

If a prospective client you met or spoke with hasn't started service yet

- Create a reminder for yourself to check in with the client if you don't hear back. Following up with clients has easily added 30-40 additional clients we wouldn't have worked with if I hadn't done so.

Keeping dogs and routes close to one another

As we've discussed there are major benefits to having clients be as close to one another as possible. Some of the benefits are:

- *Travel time*: This will lessen your travel time and that means you and your employees make more per hour.

- *Backup coverage*: When dogs are near one another it's easier to cover chaotic days. If you need to cut time on the walks to cover your day you'll need to cut much less time when the dogs on your route are near one another.

- *Maximize PR /word of mouth*: The smaller the area you're covering the more ground you can cover when it comes to street PR and word of mouth.

- *Create and maintain relationships*: In a small service area you can become the go to walker if you do a good job.

- *Maximize buildings*: If you're walking in a building with more than 1 apartment you should concentrate on the other dog owners in the building. Maybe you could start group walking some of the dogs together? Post a flier in the building and get to know fellow tenants too.

Time Frames

It's important that your clients understand your time frames. For dog walking I'd recommend having the clients choose two-hour time frames for you to arrive within (example: 10am-12pm). This means that you can arrive any time within those two hours (example: you don't have to show up by 11:30am, you can show up by 12pm).

For puppies in crates or dogs with health issues I'd recommend arriving within a one-hour time frame.

How do you decide time frames?

You should ask your clients the following:

- What time do they leave in the morning?
- What time do they come home at night?
- What time do they do a walk in the morning (if they do one)?
- What time do they do a walk in the evening (if they do one)?

Based on these answers you should be able to create a comfortable time frame for the dogs.

What if a client doesn't fit onto a route?

A client will not always fit onto a route based on the time they want and most everyone will ask for walks between 12pm-3pm. What can you do about this? Instead of getting one walk between 12pm-3pm you could recommend they get two shorter walks between 10am-12pm and 3pm-4pm or 4pm-6pm. This way the dog does not sit at home too long between walks. You can also tell the prospective client that you'll start this way and work on getting it to the one walk during the middle of the day that they originally requested.

Time between visits

The amount of time between walks in the day should not be too short or too long. A healthy adult dog should be comfortable for roughly 5 hours between walks.

Example walk: A dog is walked twice a day between 10am-12pm and

2pm-4pm. If you arrive on the later side of the time frame in the morning (12pm) then you should not arrive on the earlier side of the second time frame (2pm). You should arrive on the later side (4pm). You should space out the two walks as close to four to five hours as possible. Arriving too soon after the first walk can be as bad as arriving too late.

Puppies and dogs with health issues: As we discussed in an earlier chapter you need to space out puppy visits, especially crated dogs, based on age. When it comes to dogs with health issues you should consult with the owners about spacing out their walks.

Clients who are neurotic about time

Some clients are very neurotic when it comes to what time you arrive. It's imperative that you and your walkers reinforce your time frame structure to your clients. You can't arrive on the drop of a dime in this industry. A client who says you have to arrive at an exact time (1pm) does not understand the realities of your business. On one day you might have to spend extra time with a sick dog, while on another day you might be late because the bus was stuck in traffic. Either way you need flexibility on time when it comes to your walks. If you are arriving within a healthy time frame for the dog that is all that matters.

Note: Clients who are usually home when you arrive can be extra neurotic about time. If you usually show up at 1pm but one day show up at 1:30pm they might think something is wrong, even though you're arriving within the two-hour time frame. Do your best to educate your clients on needing time frames. If they need to change the entire two-hour time frame (or one hour time frame for puppies/dogs with health issues) that is another story but you need time frames.

A dog walking route

The following is an example of a dog walking route in our company and you can view how we arrange dogs into two hour time frames.

Bonnie:	10am- 12pm
Baxter & Cisco:	10am-12pm
Stella:	10am-12pm
Sam Diego:	11am-1pm
Michaela:	11am-1pm
Darby:	11:30am- 1:30pm
Nina:	12pm-2pm
Lou:	12pm-2pm
Oliver:	1pm-3pm
Bonnie:	2pm- 4pm
Nikki & Lexi:	2pm- 4pm
Baxter & Cisco:	3pm- 5pm
Stella:	3pm-5pm

Pet Sitter/Sleepover

Pet sitting involves taking care of a pet for someone who is out of town. This service involves most of the same skills and safety items you've already learned but there is the dynamic of the clients being gone. Pet sits can mean either a walker is sleeping at a client's home or they are taking a client's dog into their home. Here are some keys to pet sits:

- *Applications*: If you don't already you must have a completed application before you start a pet sit.

- *Emergency contacts*: Some clients do not completely fill out applications. Make sure they have filled out the emergency contacts, vet information, health information, etc.

- *Let the clients know when you arrive*: Clients are greatly relaxed by knowing when you first show up. Call, text or email them when you first arrive to let them know the pet sit has started.

- *Send them a picture of their pet*: Clients love to see a picture of their pet *happy* and *alive*.

- *Get a daily schedule*: Some clients can be very vague with what type of daily schedule they need. You want to try and mimic the daily schedule the pets are already used to.

- Have a backup plan if you or your pet sitter suddenly can't cover the pet sit.

- Have the apartment entry form with you:

- Have the vet release form on hand.

When staying in a client's home

- *Do not get curious:* Don't look in drawers, closets, don't venture anywhere that doesn't involve the care of the pet. If you're in need of something for the pet and search through areas of the house, make sure to make a note of it for the owners. If you ever break anything let the clients know immediately.

- *TV/computer*: Make sure you have permission to use the clients TV and computer before doing so.

- *Food*: Don't assume it's okay to eat the client's food or drink their wine. If the clients have not specifically told you it's okay you should assume it's not.

- *Bed*: Make sure you know what bed you're supposed to sleep on if they have more than one bed. I'd always assume it's not the master bedroom if there's more than one bed.

- *Bringing over friends*: Don't bring over friends without permission.

- *Home phone*: Don't use the client's home phone to make personal calls.

When taking a pet into your own home

- *Don't get casual*: You need to guard against getting casual when housing a pet in your home. You need to make sure that the same professionalism applies that you would show in a client's home.

- *Other people in your home*: Do you or your sitters have a roommate? If so make sure they don't bother the pet and definitely make sure they don't take it out for a walk.

- *More than one pet at a time*: I personally would not recommend housing more than one pet at a time, unless they already know each other well. If you do house more than one dog you'll need to supervise them even more than normal.

- *Daytime visits*: Whether your pet sitters have daytime jobs or not you need to maintain the normal daytime schedules. That might require that you have a second walker do the daytime visits while the pet sitters are gone. If this is needed you should arrange it ahead of time.

- *Copies of pet sitters' keys*: With that said if you are a purely pet sitting business you'll still need dog walkers for the daytime walks if your sitters are gone. This will also require you to have a copy of each pet sitter's home keys for backup coverage and emergencies.

Note: If you are purely a pet sitting company you still should check in on your sitters as much as you would a daily dog walker. What's a good way to keep checks and balances with a pet sitter keeping a pet in his or her home? If they are keeping a dog in their home ask them to meet you nearby while on the walk with the dog. Make this like a check-in where you get to see the sitter walking but you also get to make sure they walk a decent distance with the dog.

Note: You should check with your insurance carriers (NAPPS, PSI, etc.) to find out their policy on taking pets into your own home. If you haven't already you will most likely have pay an additional fee to have your policy cover pets in your own home. If you don't have this coverage and something goes wrong in your home, you could be liable if the dog were to get injured or sick inside your home.

End of chapter checklist

- Decide what your rates will be.
- Raise rates over time.
- Phone etiquette.
- Prepare for what new clients might ask you.
- Qualify clients to make sure they are right for your service.
- Be prepared when you meet new clients.
- Close clients.
- Stay on top of clients who have not yet committed to service.
- Keep dogs and routes as close to one another as possible.
- Make sure clients understand your time frames.
- Prepare for pet sits.

Chapter 9

Customer Service, Good Clients, Bad Clients, Managing Client Issues

The honeymoon period

Okay, so your marketing has worked, you've met your clients and now they are starting. Now it's time to relax, right? Not at all! You need to be hypersensitive to your clients' needs for the first few weeks of service. Getting hired is not the end of the process of impressing your clients. It's just the beginning. Small mistakes will be greatly intensified in those first few weeks, big mistakes even more so.

Try and be perfect as you always will but show even more sensitivity to things that might seem small to you but could be misconstrued by a client (not drying down the dog and subsequently the dog gets dirt all over the floor; using the client's bathroom without asking; forgetting to feed the dog; forgetting to do anything at all). Deal with these things immediately – show a great concern for the clients' issues and take steps to assure them it will not happen again.

- *Small problems are not always so small*: A note from an owner reminding you to do something they have already asked you to do, can be a serious issue. You can't assume they are writing the note in a calm, supportive nature. They might have been grinding the pen into the pad to write the note. Take owner requests very seriously, especially when they are reminders.

Customer service

Running a pet service requires strong attention to detail and excellent customer service skills. I mean just think about the unique dynamic of running a pet service. You are providing service to animals whose owners will rarely if ever see you perform your job. But even though the client doesn't see you perform your job they will still develop an opinion of the job you are doing. A big part of that opinion will be based on how good the customer service you provide them is.

Customer Service? We don't give no stinking customer service!

"In the old days, dealers knew your name, what you drank, what you played. Today, it's like checkin' into an airport. And if you order room service, you're lucky if you get it by Thursday."

- ROBERT DeNIRO IN THE MOVIE - CASINO

You don't have to go very far to experience bad customer service. Just think about it for a moment. How often do you receive good customer service? When you call your cable company? When you go out to dinner? When you call your property manager? If you routinely receive good customer service than you're in the minority because polls show customer service has become very poor in this country. Because I provide customer service to my clients for a living, I have a unique view to judge the customer service I receive. I am routinely dumbfounded at how poor it usually is.

So what can you do about this with your company? A lot! From the very beginning you can set a tone with your company of providing a high level of customer service to separate yourself from your competition and from the expectations of many of your clients. Astound your clients with the high quality of customer service you provide. This doesn't mean you should let clients walk all over you; it just means when a client has a legitimate complaint or concern make sure you address it in the manner you would like your own concerns answered.

Every time I have a bad experience with customer service, and they are plentiful, I promise myself that I need to offer better service with my own clients. If there's anything good about how bad customer support in this country has gotten it's that it will be easier for your company to stand out with good customer service.

What is good customer service?

To me, good customer service is an acknowledgement of your customer's complaint even if you don't agree with it. The fact that your customer is upset is important enough in itself to register your interest and some type of resolution. That resolution might range from an apology to an explanation to a company- wide policy change.

When your explanation is not enough to satisfy a client

You've talked to your client numerous times on the phone, exchanged emails, and have taken your walker to task but they are still not happy! What do you do?

First, I would ask myself if this is a good client? A big client? An irrational client?

If a client is impossible to please and has irrational complaints, you should do your best but part ways if it starts to drain you.

Common client complaints/concerns

- Not getting full walk time.
- Was walker actually there?
- Not walking the dog hard enough.
- Coming out of walk time frames (10am-12pm, etc.).
- Dog not getting socialized.
- Dog barking while they're gone.
- Dog not getting enough exercise.
- Dog going to the bathroom in the house.
- Walker using the bathroom (and the water running afterwards).
- Walker forgetting to sign in.
- Dog picking things up off the ground.
- Dog being given treats that aren't owner approved.
- Dog going to dog run/playing with others dogs without owner's approval.

Clients who are overly skeptical of you and/or your walker

I have found that those who can't trust others are themselves hard to trust. People with this personality always feel they are owed more and you can never please them, no matter what you do. And you know what, you shouldn't try and please them because it's a fool's errand.

Clients vs. walkers

What a tough position to be in. You need your clients and you need your walkers, and to have a client complaining about a walker or vice versa puts you in a tough spot. A good walker is more of a rare commodity than a good client. Both a good client and a good employee should be appreciated but don't immediately throw a good walker away for one mistake, or at least a mistake a client finds to be a bigger deal than you do.

Situations with Complaints

- Your client thinks something happened.

- Your client knows something happened.

- Your client knows something happened and it's happened before but they didn't tell you last time.

- You witness the issue with your own eyes.

- A fellow walker tells you about the problem.

- A doorman, super or 3rd party witnesses the issue.

Clients vs. You (the office)

A client directing complaints at you can be an especially confusing situation and hopefully this is a very rare thing. Luckily for me I can count on one hand the number of clients who have verbalized any issues with me specifically. Complaints are almost always in regard to some area of service, the walker and/or billing. Consider the following when a client complains about you or the office:

- Is the client right in what they are complaining about? No matter how you feel about the client you can use this as an opportunity to learn from their feedback and maybe even improve your service based on their complaint. Never have too much pride to not improve your service just because it's coming from a client or person you don't like.

- Is this a good client? Do they appreciate the service you provide? Are they a fan of your service, your philosophies and/or you personally?

- Are they a bad client? Do they consistently try and push you to do things you don't want to? Do they show no appreciation for your service?

- Do they appreciate the way you try and run your business?

I will say that most clients who have specifically complained about me (made things personal as opposed to professional) were clients who did not appreciate my service nor realize what a large role I played in the daily life of their walkers. Some clients are not right for your company. Sometimes you should do yourself a favor and get rid of bad clients who do nothing but complain, show neither appreciation for your service nor for the effort you are putting into the company. Don't rid yourself of all such people, but do get rid of the ones who suck up 5-7 times more of your energy than a regular client. They're not worth it and getting rid of them will free you to get even more and better clients into your business.

What pet service clients seem to appreciate

- Lots of feedback.
- Honesty.
- Professional walkers.
- Personal approach.
- Images, videos and written feedback on their pets.
- A guiding hand with their dogs' problems.
- Showing true concern for their pets' issues and/or the client's own.
- Sure you might not normally offer night walks but if a client has a personal emergency you should do everything possible to cover this walk (by emergency I mean sickness, injury, death, etc.)

Don't give your clients a reason to leave

Your clients do not want to leave your company. Most people would rather not have the need to once again have to find someone to entrust with their home and pets. They *want* to trust you, and being entrusted with someone's home and pets is a big responsibility. You need to do everything possible not to lose that trust, and if there is the smallest indication of losing it you need to address the situation (especially if this is a good client, this is where you provide hotel//casino customer service). It is a jungle out there in regard to the competition. Your clients want to value you. You need to make them comfortable enough to do just that.

Clients are great BUT I have found the majority of them love whichever walker is in front of them presently, and by that I mean they will forget their past walker quickly. With that said, keep them in your company. They don't want to have to interview multiple other walkers and start the process all over again in order to develop a comfort level with someone else. Do what you need to do to keep them in your company.

Good customer service

Good customer service seems to be something of a lost art form in this country. More and more people seem to be most interested in what someone can do for them and that doesn't lend itself to good customer service.

What do I consider good customer service? To me good customer service first involves acknowledging a client's complaint even if you don't agree with it. A client's complaint is important to them, important enough to contact you, so don't dismiss it and don't immediately try to rebut it. At the very least, show an appreciation for the client raising the issue and tell them you are going to investigate the issue and give them an explanation. And make sure to do just that! Acknowledging a client's complaint is just the start. You need to follow up and answer the client's complaint, give them some type of resolution or credit if deserved, and also explain some type of action plan to try and avoid it happening again. See the big picture: you want to keep this client in your company! And even if you don't want them there you don't want them to leave with a negative opinion of your company.

Bad customer service

Nothing will lose a client faster than bad customer service. After all your hard work of getting a client into your company then to lose them over lack of communication or poor communication? If a client is worth keeping in your company you need to make sure to answer their concerns and/or foresee their concerns. To me, bad customer service includes some of the following:

- Not acknowledging the client's concern.

- Immediately arguing with the client.

- Not responding at all.

- Acknowledging the client's concern but not following up on it.

- Acknowledging and following up on a client's concern but not learning what to avoid in the future.

- Forcing a client to encounter the same problem over and over.

- Having poor systems to voice concerns.

- Having slow response times.

- Being rude.

- Not seeing the big picture.

Don't let things fester in a client's mind

If you're concerned that you've had a misunderstanding with a client don't let things fester. Try and react to issues quickly and if necessary offer a client a free walk or some extra time to make them happy.

Email vs. talking on the phone

Email is great for a lot of things except for serious problems you're having with a client. An email can be ripe for misunderstanding. Things written by you with one intention can be taken completely differently by the reader. It can be easier to get across your point through a phone call or in person. I'd avoid saying anything strong through an email.

Look at things in percentages

Here is some advice that I hope will guide you through both the relationship with your clients and your employees. The advice is to *look at things in percentages*. What do I mean by that? You need to create boundaries in all areas of your business. These boundaries constitute acceptable barriers that you do not want to cross.

Examples

- *I can't have more than (percent) of neurotic clients.*
- *I can't have more than (percent) of high maintenance employees.*
- *My company can't take more than (percent) in total losses.*
- *I can't have more than (percent) of clients who take up too much of my time.*

How does looking at areas of your business in percentages help you? First of all it allows you to de-personalize a situation.

Example: A walker does not return the equipment you gave them to use on the job.

The equipment only costs $80 but you are so incensed by the rudeness of the walker not returning the equipment you make it a personal venture to get the equipment back. You call the walker repeatedly, email the walker repeatedly and even start leaving angry messages on the walker's voicemail. And for what? $80 in equipment?

Now what if instead of concentrating on who didn't return what and the emotional side of the equation you just looked at the loss of the $80 on a spreadsheet with no names, just numbers. You took a loss of $80 on the equipment, which brings your acceptable amount of loss for the year up to what? If it's well within the acceptable amount of loss for your company then just forget it and move on. Be happy you no longer have to deal with that employee anymore. You and your company are better off without him or her. And what if this $80 in lost equipment takes you over your acceptable loss for this year? What should you do then? Study the situation at hand and figure out what changes need to be made to stay within your accepted limits. To rectify the problem I just described when the $80 equipment was not returned? To protect myself against it, I took an equipment deposit that my employees get back once the equipment is returned.

This philosophy of looking at things in percentages should come in handy when you're going through periods of not loving your clients. Are your clients really so bad? Or is it just a few bad apples? Are there more bad apples than you can handle? Do the amount of bad apples exceed your acceptable amount of bad apples? If so maybe you should get rid of a few of them. It will make you happier and the time you don't now need to spend on this client can be spent on other more deserving clients and/or on getting new clients.

It's inevitable that you will go through highs and lows in how you feel about your clients. What I'd like you to try and do from the very beginning is see your clients, and all aspects of your business actually, in percentages. Meaning how many bad clients you can have, how many clients can be behind on their bills, how many clients can be overly neurotic, etc. You need to create boundaries that you will not allow others to cross and if they do you need to respond. You need to respond to keep your business in order but more importantly you need to respond to keep your self in order.

- I'll accept a loss of 5% in the company (clients not paying, equipment being lost or not returned, etc.)
- I'll accept a certain amount of high maintenance clients.
- I'll allow clients to vent their frustrations to a certain point.
- I'll allow clients to do things outside of our policies to what point.

And how do you decide what that point is? Some of these answers can be based on industry standards like 5-7% loss is accepted by most businesses. But more often than not the answer of how much is going to be decided by your personal comfort level. This is something I want you to work with and while you're not going to come up with all the answers now, you will over time.

How looking at percentages helps you deal with problems

Problems are going to occur, it's just a fact of life. How you look at these problems and respond might very well determine how successful you will be with this business. It might be cliché but problems really are a blessing in that they can expose a weakness in your company. I've had people angrily point something out about my business and I've later been thankful to them because they pointed something out to me when it was a small problem. I listened to what this angry person was saying and not how they were saying it. I learned from it, fixed the problem, and my company is better off for it.

Looking at problems as percentages allows you to look at the issues as a number on a paper and not as a personal slight against you. There are bumps in the road, some people will disappoint you but you'll get used to the bumps and will grow to not fear them.

Good Clients vs. Bad Clients

A *good client* is one who values the services you offer and cares about their pet. A good client might be difficult but fair and particular but rational. A good client will accept your apology for a mistake, but many will expect it not to happen again.

A *bad client* is one who does not value your services and tries to push you away from your business plan. A bad client does not show any interest in your policies, even after you politely remind them on a few occasions. A bad client is

irrational, doesn't care about the welfare of his or her pet, consistently does not pay on time and is condescending.

Friends of mine always want to know about the famous clients we've had. I tell them *my* famous clients are the ones whose credit cards go through every week. What this means is that we don't care about someone's popularity. The clients we cater to the most are the ones who are diligent and keep up with payments and with their dogs.

Should you work with bad clients who happen to be big money clients? You need to decide what type of pain you can shoulder. We all have our own pet peeves—some can't stand clients who don't pay attention to the company's policies, others can't stand overly neurotic clients. I personally ended service with a client whose lifestyle completely contradicted my animal welfare beliefs. The point is not to be afraid to rid yourself of problem clients (and walkers) who can warp your perception of all the other great clients you have.

Clients loving their walkers, but not you

This is a confusing situation to be in but you will very likely experience it. The walkers are the ones in the clients' homes, walking their dogs, etc. They don't always understand how much impact you have on the quality of their service. Here are some suggestions to combat this issue:

- *Allegiance*: Make sure your walkers' allegiance is to you and not the clients. Also make sure the walkers understand they work for you and not the clients. Having the allegiance of your walkers is the simplest, easiest way to keep your clients in line. It's imperative that the clients contact you in the office to address issues with service and not the walkers.

- *Keep walkers in line*: Often the making of a bad client is a bad walker engaging the client outside of what your policies dictate. Gently remind your walkers to help you keep the clients in line. If a walker engages with clients in a way that cause you problems you'll need to consider letting this walker go.

- *Educate yourself*: As I've mentioned, your knowledge of dog issues and your ability to help your clients with their dog's issues will earn their appreciation.

- *Educate your clients*: Make sure your clients understand everything it is that you do for them. List pages on your website where they can learn more about what goes on behind the scenes with your service. Even clients who didn't seem to value my role in the company did seem to understand how difficult it was to find, screen, train and manage good employees.

- *Stay in touch:* Whether it be through email, letters, phone, Twitter or a bit of all of them, do make it a point to stay in your clients' ears.

- *Stay personal:* Make sure you get to know all the dogs in your company.

Meet all dogs in person, take pictures and videos of them and get to know the problems they have so you can help solve them.

- *Don't take it personally*: It's hard not to take it personally when your clients don't value the work you do for them but it's in your personal and professional interest not to! Remember to look at things in percentages and to remove the visual of this client from your mind. Are they one of a handful of clients that don't appreciate you? If so maybe you can deal with a few clients like that in your company. But in the end do what is best for you and your company and sometimes that means parting ways with a client.

It seems like the clients are always just telling me what to do!

The client is, well, the client. But don't lose sight of the fact that they are telling you what to do within *your* guidelines. You need to have these guidelines in place and if they work and you believe in them, you need to stick to them. Allow your client to vent about his or her issues but have boundaries that can't be crossed. I have always allowed my clients to vent as much as they want but I have not allowed them to get disrespectful with me or with my employees.

When issues arise: communicate, communicate and communicate

You need to be engaged with your clients, your employees and those you do business with in general. Don't let your referral partners lose track of you, stay fresh in their minds with phone calls, emails, a small present of thanks, etc. You need to also stay fresh in your clients' minds. Let them know what's going on inside your company. Tell them of action plans to add services and features in the future. Give them the opportunity to submit their own ideas for your company. Your employees will not be in front of you as they perform their work most of the time, but make sure they always know you're there. Pop in on them, require lots of feedback from them and nudge them (if they need nudging) to remind them you're there. Maybe you're not physically out there on the route with them but make them feel as if you are.

- When a problem arises deal with it quickly, swiftly and fairly. When dealing with a problem, always see the big picture and which is - you want to keep the customer here. Your customers don't want to have to get a new dog walker so don't give them the opportunity to.
- If a client is unhappy with a walk, maybe give them a credit for the walk?

Don't charge them for that walk. It could be the difference between losing a client of 3-4 years vs. crediting them $15. When a client is right provide them "hotel" customer service. Maybe you won't be giving them a bottle of champagne and tickets to a show, but a free walk or free extra time on the next walk is a dog walker's version of "hotel" customer service.

Clients I have decided not to work with/kicked out of my company

- Clients who show no interest in my policies and yet are endless with their requests and neurosis.
- Clients who are exceedingly rude to my walkers.
- Clients who ask me to go against my company's beliefs or even worse, my own beliefs.
- Clients who expect us to be run like a real company but resent us for actually doing so (raising prices, having policies, etc.).

How do you ask a client to leave your company?

I'm going to be honest with you here, don't be honest when you part ways with your clients! Up until recently I have always been honest with clients I don't think we can work with and it has brought me nothing but stress and aggravation. Why? Some clients can't believe that their pet service is actually parting ways with *them*. I have had clients curse at me and threaten me, among other things when parting ways with them. Am I telling you to lie when parting ways with a bad client? Yes, for your sake I am telling you to tell a white lie to part ways. Tell them the walker can no longer cover them on the route, or they are out of your service area, or you're ending the route, etc. Do what's best for you and your company here but *always* make sure to give clients plenty of notice to find a new walker. The last thing you'd want to do is have this client's dog start getting walked by a terrible dog walker. No matter how you feel about the client you should still feel responsible for giving this client time to find a new walker. I think giving a client 4-6 weeks is more than enough time for them to find a new service.

What if I don't agree with how my clients treat their pets?

This is a very tricky situation to be in. It's a certainty that you will have some clients who treat their pets badly. Some clients will be verbally abusive to their pets but you might even run into a client who smacks his or her pet. I'd first try and figure out the situation on your own. Try and show the client other ways to deal with the pet. But If the situation is not something you can handle I'd call the local ASPCA. Overall though I've always felt it's better that I'm involved with the pet of a bad owner than someone else who might not care. I've had a lot of success helping bad owners do better with their pets. I've never worked with an abusive owner and I hope you never have to.

Don't fall in love with your clients

What I mean by this is don't ever lose sight of the fact that you are running a business. Your clients, as much as you might grow to like them, are your clients. What I have found to consistently be the case is your clients love whoever their present dog walker happens to be. If they get a new dog walker, they are going to love that person and soon forget the past walker. I have clients who grow to love their present walker so much they almost refuse to accept a different walker from me. But once they do accept a different walker they usually fall in love with the new walker and then I go through the whole process again! My point? Enjoy your interactions with your clients because much might come from them. But outside of very rare occasions, your clients are not your friends, they are your clients and you shouldn't fall in love with them. Knowing this ahead of time will lessen the blow when clients disappoint you. And clients *will* disappoint you over time.

When clients disappoint you

Now we've already discussed looking at your problems in percentages and how you should never fall in love with your clients. Both of these ideas are meant to help you best deal with clients who let you down and/or are disloyal. It's unfortunate but it's just about guaranteed this will happen. No matter how hard you work. No matter how good the service you offer is. No matter how honest you are. It won't matter to some clients. I've had clients whom I've loved as clients who have left me for walkers who any day now I fear I'll hear got the dog hurt or even worse. To me it was insanity and betrayal but that's also because I was taking it personally and I'd let myself fall in love with them as clients. If you're running around at 11 p.m. at night doing short-notice walks for a dog, don't do it because you want the love of your clients. Do it because you love animals and to please the clients on a business level. Unless your client has become a true friend of yours whom you hang out with outside of the job, only push your limits because it makes you happy to care for the dog and/or for the benefit of your business. And don't expect the love of your clients for doing everything they ask – expect them to be happy customers.

But for those rare clients who are huge champions of your service and are true friends to you and your company? Value them, as the following passage describes:

> *"He remembered a story he'd once heard about a girl throwing starfish into the ocean. 'An old man comes along and says to her, 'Don't bother. There's millions of them out here. You can't save them. What you're doing won't make a difference.' She looks at the starfish in her hand and says, 'It makes a difference to this one.' And she throws it into the ocean."*

> - FROM SMALL GIANTS, COMPANIES THAT CHOOSE TO BE GREAT INSTEAD OF GOOD

End of chapter checklist

- Be overly attentive to your client's needs in the first month.
- Offer great customer service.
- Don't let bad thoughts fester in a client's mind.
- Look at problems in percentages.
- Value those clients who show appreciation for your service.
- Don't fall in love with your clients.

Chapter 10

Preparing for Walkers, Setting Up Routes, Setting Up Backup Coverage, Finding Walkers

It's the walkers stupid

"It's the economy, stupid!" is a quote made famous during the 1992 presidential campaign, but for owners of a pet service, the quote would be, "it's the walkers, stupid!" You can have the coolest website and the most brilliant marketing strategy but if you don't have great walkers it's all for nothing. Your greatest commodity as a pet service is the quality of your dog walkers. There's no better feeling than knowing you have a team of dog walking ninjas working for you whom you completely trust. On the flip side there's nothing worse than having doubts about those who work for you, let alone the financial ramifications from walkers who don't work out. Think about it, you're allowing someone into your clients' apartments, to walk their dogs and represent you and your company name. That is a big responsibility and you must take it very seriously. Hiring great walkers and training them well is also one of the best ways to separate yourself from your competition.

Before you hire your first walker

Before you hire your first walker I recommend you do the following:

- Hire a lawyer to consult with you on labor policies in your state.
- Create the strongest agreements possible that your lawyer says can be enforced in your state.
- Create a company handbook listing all of your policies.
- Decide how much you'll pay your walkers.
- Sign up for a payroll service.
- Talk to your accountant or lawyer about how to get worker's compensation and disability insurance.

Hire a good lawyer

I recommend that you involve a lawyer before hiring the first person to work with you. There are simply too many things to know about labor laws in your state not to involve a professional. Some of the things a lawyer will advise you on:

- Should your walkers be independent contractors or employees?
- If your lawyer advises you to go with independent contractors how should you treat your walkers? What can you and can you not tell them to do? (It's very important to know these answers!)
- Should your company be an LLC or a Corporation (this can also be answered by your accountant)?

- Do you need to get worker's compensation and disability insurance (almost assuredly yes)?

- Should you be charging sales tax on all transactions (another question your accountant could also answer)?

- Does your state allow for non-compete agreements? Non-disclosure agreements?

- As well as the many other questions you will run into along the way. How much will a lawyer cost you to answer these questions? I'd say anywhere from $250-$1,000 depending on how many questions you have and how long you talk. But you will also need a lawyer to draft a non-compete and nondisclosure (if they are allowed in your state) and this could cost an additional $1,000 or more. Seems like a lot of money right? The power of having this advice and the strongest legal forms possible is worth *much* more than what you will pay. Proceeding *without* knowing the answers to the questions I've raised could very well lead to the *downfall of your business*!

Tip: Try and make a budget with a lawyer *before* you start working together. Make an agreement not to go over your budget and for them to not charge for things you're not aware of. Don't be shy about saying this is a lot of money for you but you'd like to build a long relationship with the lawyer.

Another tip: Don't be afraid to stop working with your lawyer, accountant, web designer, etc. if you're not happy with them. There are others you can work with. I've made the mistake of working with people much longer than I should have because of the worry of finding someone new. Once I made the change I found *much better* people to work with.

And another tip: Unless you are a lawyer do not write up your own agreements. If you don't know labor law you will likely add something that makes the entire agreement invalid.

From this point forward

Going forward I will discuss potential walkers and existing walkers as if they were employees because that's how I run my business. If you and your lawyer or accountant have decided to classify your walkers as independent contractors you'll need to make sure what I recommend applies to you.

Company Handbook

Before you hire your first walker you should create a *company handbook*. In this handbook you want to jot down all the important guidelines you want your walkers to follow. These policies might include some of the following:

- Always follow the client's safety guidelines.
- Never walk a dog off leash.
- Never take a dog to a dog run without permission.
- Never group walk a client's dog unless the client has given permission.

This is just a small sample of some of the items you can include. The point is that your company handbook should cover all the main areas of servicing dogs. The walkers should have to sign your handbook and acknowledge your policies. If you ever need to fire a walker it will be a big help if you can document that the walker has violated the policies in your company handbook. But a company handbook is also another good way to try and ensure quality in your walkers.

A bad walker is the single most costly thing that can happen to your business. A bad walker can lose existing business and future business too. Insulate your business as much as possible from bad walkers.

Sign up for a payroll service

If you, your lawyer and accountant decided to classify your walkers as employees, you'll need to sign up for *a payroll service* and you'll need *to take taxes out of the walkers' checks*. A payroll service submits your payroll numbers to the IRS. I would *highly suggest* using a payroll service and not doing this yourself. If you decided to use Quickbooks as your accounting software you can use Quickbooks' own payroll service and it will sync directly with your software. I would recommend Quickbooks' payroll service in general though and you can learn more at: *www.payroll.intuit.com*.

If you don't classify your walkers as employees: Please involve the services of an accountant to advise you what to do.

When is the right time to hire your first walker?

I never set out to create a dog walking company, more than my own route that is. If you're reading this chapter, then you have an interest in growing your company to more than just yourself. Here are some key factors in deciding the right time to hire your first employee:

- *Income*: Make sure you can withstand a hit to your personal income. When you add your first walker you will inevitably make less at first.

- *Make sure your own route is busting at the seams:* Have your own route be so full with clients that you can barely cover it. This way you can give the person you hire one half to two-thirds of your route to get started. And you can take the remaining dogs and work on your next route!

- *Prepare your office*: Have your office super organized. Make sure you charge your cell phone every night and that you sync your cell phone every morning to add new contact information, calendar events, etc.

- *Be prepared for things to get more stressful*: Having to walk your own route, manage another walker (and in the future manage multiple walkers) will be stressful at first. Prepare yourself psychologically to take on this increased burden.

- *There is never a perfect time to grow*: We all wait for that perfect time to start our own business, take the leap, etc. We all want things to line up perfectly between leaving our old job and starting our new one. Often things don't work out this way. Hiring your first walker and future walkers is a huge investment in your company and your own future.

Keeping routes close to one another

There is huge power in having routes be close to one another. If one walker needs help on his or her route, gets sick, is running behind, has the day off, etc. the walker nearby can easily help out. If two routes are near each other and are both part-time routes, you can likely combine the two routes very easily if the walker leaves on short notice for another job. I can't stress enough the benefit of having routes near one another. You can actually attribute your ability to grow your company to the proximity of one route to another.

Backup walkers

To grow a pet service it's imperative that you have backup plans in place to cover the routes when your regular walkers get sick, go on vacations, etc. We'll discuss backup coverage in greater detail later but for now take a look at the following images that detail backup coverage.

Growing Routes

Over the next few pages you'll find images that visually show you how routes can be set up. I hope this helps you see the benefits of setting up routes close to one another and the pitfalls of not doing so.

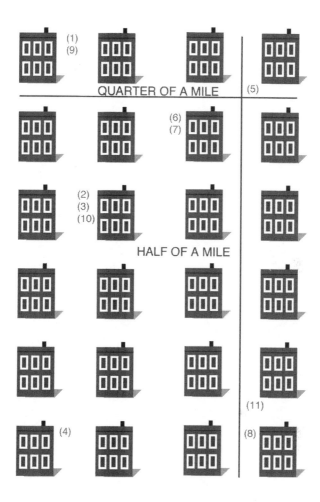

Figure 1A   Example of a city route that is set up badly

In this example the walker will walk a few miles in a single day just to reach their dogs, let alone the walks they do with the dogs. If you notice the distance between 1/9 to 8/11/4, the walker will most likely need to take a bus or ride a bike to reach their walks on time. A route like this has lots of unpaid time for the walker or if you pay hourly you will be paying the walker for hours when they are not brining in income.

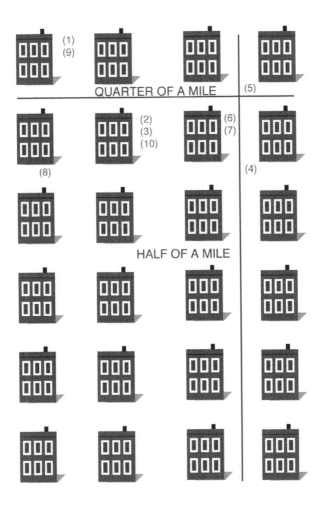

Figure 1B A City route that is set up well.

In this example most walks are within 3-4 blocks of each other and this increases the amount of money the walker/the office will make per hour. Keeping dogs near one another also allows you to do more walks in a day, makes your walkers happier and probably ensures that your walkers will stay with you longer.

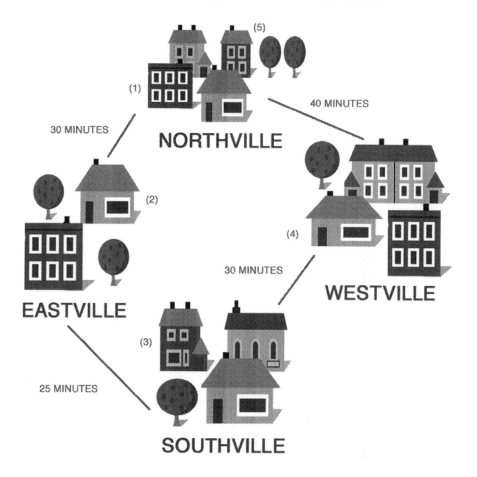

Figure 1C A route in the country that is not set up well.

If you notice the walker needs to travel to 4 different neighborhoods to cover the route. Their travel time amounts to over 2 hours and that will also increase the amount they need to spend on gas each day or time they'll be on public transportation. If something goes wrong in their travels, a traffic jam, accident, etc. their route might not even be done in time.

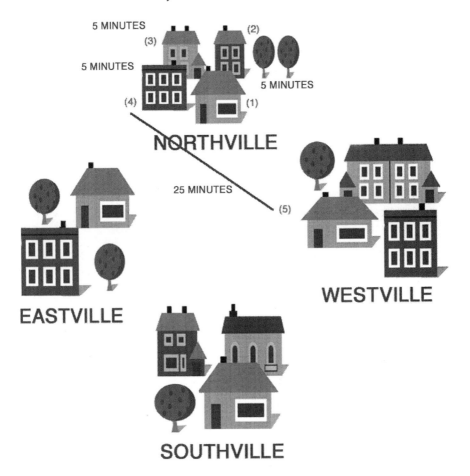

5 MINUTES
(3)
(2)

5 MINUTES
5 MINUTES
(4)
(1)

NORTHVILLE

25 MINUTES
(5)

WESTVILLE

EASTVILLE

SOUTHVILLE

Figure 1D This is an example of a route in the country that is set up well.

Four out of the five walks on this route are within 5 minutes of each other and that provides flexibility if the walker is running behind.

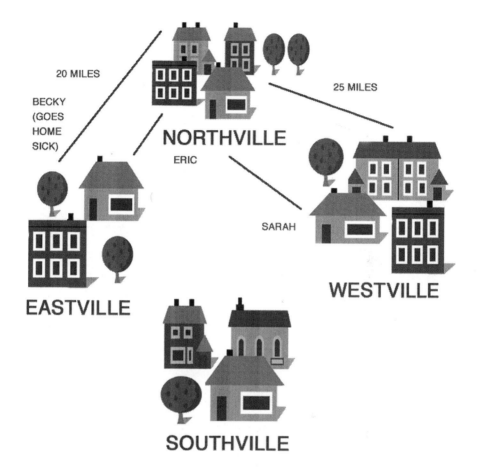

20 MILES

BECKY
(GOES
HOME
SICK)

NORTHVILLE

ERIC

25 MILES

SARAH

EASTVILLE

WESTVILLE

SOUTHVILLE

Figure 1E   Backup coverage in the country where the backup walkers are far from each other.

As you can see a walker named Becky has become sick and she's going home early. The closest walker to Becky is Eric who is over 20 miles away. Eric is going to rush over to cover Becky's walks but then he needs Sarah to cover his own walks. Sarah is 25 miles away from Eric's route and to cover both routes she's going to need to go very short on her walk times, so short that some clients might get upset. This type of coverage scheme is chaotic, tough on the walkers, tough on the dogs and will likely upset/lose clients over time.

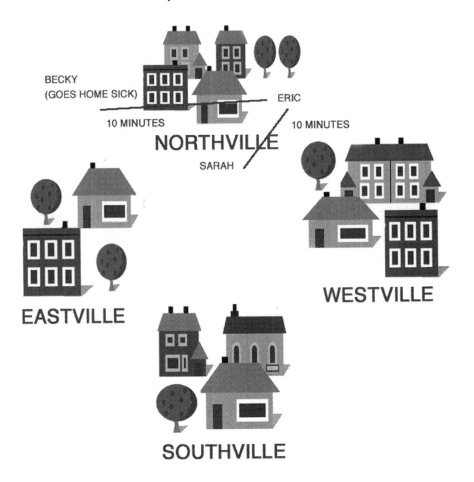

BECKY
(GOES HOME SICK)

ERIC

10 MINUTES

10 MINUTES

NORTHVILLE

SARAH

WESTVILLE

EASTVILLE

SOUTHVILLE

Figure 1F   Backup coverage in the country where the routes are near each other.

This example in the country has Becky going home early because she's sick. In this example Eric and Sarah, the backup walkers, are so close that they can both take on a few of Becky's walks. If Eric or Sarah have cancellations that day, they might not even need to cut time on any of their visits. Either way though they will be able to cut much less time if they need to because they are both close to Becky's route. This proximity of route to another will make clients, walkers and dogs happier and lead to you making more money too.

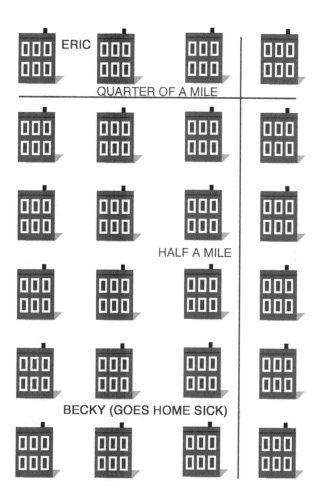

Figure 1G Backup coverage in a city where the routes aren't near each other.

Becky is going home early because she's sick. The closest walker to Becky is Eric who is over half a mile away on foot. The only way Eric can cover both his and Becky's dogs is to cut drastic amounts of times on the visits. As we've already discussed this will be chaotic for everyone involved and could lead to lost business over time as well.

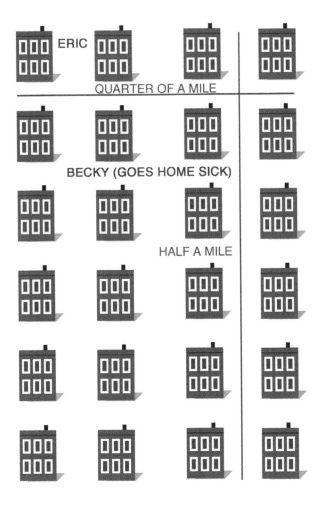

Figure 1H Backup coverage in a city where the routes are near each other.

Becky is going home sick but her backup, Eric, works close by. If Eric has any dogs off his route today he might not even need to shorten his walks to cover Becky's route. But even if he does need to cut time it will be much less time than in the prior example.

So what's the point? There are huge benefits in keeping dogs close to one another on a route. There are also huge benefits to keeping each route close to other routes.

Note: You might ask, "why not just keep a walker on call who can cover walks when needed?" I've tried this before and what I've found is walkers who don't walk daily don't do as good a job as those who do. The job takes a lot of concentration and you might be hard pressed to find a reliable backup walker who can perform the job nearly as well as your daily dog walkers. If you have a walker on call, you will still need to backup your routes from within your daily walkers.

Hiring and managing walkers

I don't know your managerial history but no matter your experience I promise you can do this. I have had success in having walkers stay, in the quality of the walkers and in their loyalty. Some keys to that success are:

- Loyalty: I am a loyal person and I've had many walkers tell me they appreciate how much I've supported them.

- *Treat them with respect*: Most dog walkers I've hired are in between careers. While I consider dog walking to be a very respectable and rewarding job, there are those who look down on it and make fun of it as a job. I have found it very important to treat my walkers with respect both for their self-esteem and also to earn their respect.

- *Provide a living wage*: It's important that you know the financial requirements *before* you hire a walker. Make sure that you can provide enough income for the walker to make a healthy living. But also make sure the walker isn't going to expect a level of income you can't provide them.

- *Be generous*: I have always tried to reward my walkers as best I could. Sometimes it was with a Starbucks gift certificate, while other times it was a paid day off. During the holidays I have given my walkers jackets for the winter time and walking sneakers during the warm months. I also think you should also reward walkers who put extra effort in the job. In the beginning maybe give small touches like Chapstick or gel insoles and increase the cost of your gifts over time.

- *Don't be too generous*: There was a time when I used to give paid sick days, no matter how many a walker took. I would add extra money to the walkers' checks no matter how much they made. I spent many hundreds of dollars on each of my walker's holiday gifts. And you know what? It was during the times I lavished the most on my walkers that they seemed to appreciate it the least.

- *See the walkers often and in person*: It doesn't matter if you're out dog walking everyday or at home running the office, you need to see your walkers in person. And more importantly you need to see your walkers with the animals. You can't base your opinion of how your walkers perform their job by how they sound on the phone or through email. A walker's phone personality or email writing is often not reflective at all of the job they are doing with the animals. You or someone working for you needs to see the walkers performing their jobs in person. As they saying goes, "trust but verify" your walkers.

How much should you pay walkers?

Hopefully you already thought about this *before deciding* how much to charge your clients. Again it's imperative that your price point supports your being able to pay your walkers fairly and also make enough for yourself. Then you need to decide in what way you will pay your walkers.

To decide how much you should pay your walkers you'll need to consider the following:

- Do you want to pay them per dog or per hour?
- What are your competitors paying their walkers?
- What are your fixed costs?

Will you pay them per dog? Per hour? Per dog on an hourly rate? Keep in mind that your walkers will learn how much you charge the clients over time. If you decide to pay your walkers a low hourly rate but also charge the clients a high price point, your walkers might get angry. You also need to decide if you will pay your walkers for down time. If they have a gap in their schedule will you assume responsibility for the down time? Or will you only pay them an hourly rate for when they are actually walking dogs? Rates paid to dog walkers is another area in which you should study the competition. Ask around and see what other companies pay their walkers.

Paying per dog vs. hourly...

I've always paid my walkers per dog because I feel it gives them an incentive to work. They realize that the more they work the more they get paid. Whereas when you pay hourly the walkers might be counting the dogs they are walking wondering how much you are making off them. In terms of what works out better financially for you or the walkers I'm not sure. If you have an active client base I would think you would do better financially by paying hourly. But again you risk resentment from your walkers who might think you're taking advantage of them.

What are your competitors paying their walkers?

This is pretty easy to find out. Look at your competitor's websites or call them up directly and ask them. Try and get feedback from a wide variety of competitors, from high end to low end, etc. Then you need to decide what type of service you

want to be. Do you want to offer exceptional customer service and coverage for a high-end clientele and high price point? Or do you want to offer lower prices with pack walking and a less personal approach to try and get as many customers as possible? I'm not a fan of pack walking myself but I know some good walkers who walk 3-4 dogs at a time but never more. You need to think about the above and decide what fits your personality best. The higher end clientele will bring with it more demands and expectations of you and less tolerance for a change in walkers.

What I did: I decided to offer individual dog walking with the option of a second dog if the owner requested it. My price point has not been the most expensive nor the cheapest. I've tried to stay roughly in between the two. This has allowed me to attract clients of both sides. I've attracted those looking for a decent price and they find all the extra perks here an added bonus. We've also attracted the high-end client looking for a little bit of everything.

What I did wrong: At first my price point was too low based on what I was paying and giving my walkers. Don't forget about yourself! You're in this business for the love of it but also to make money!

What are your fixed costs?

A mistake I made in the beginning of this company was not factoring in my fixed costs when it came to what I was paying my walkers. Fixed costs are costs you have to pay like insurance, workers compensation, payroll etc. Your unfixed costs are things you choose to invest in like PR materials, a new computer, advertising, etc. In the beginning of my payroll was too high in relation to my prices to make a good profit. Once I increased the rates, just $1, my profit margin drew tremendously. Make sure you study and keep track of your costs in relation to your profit. Many people have no idea what their costs or profits are. Remember it's not how much money you make, it's how much money you keep.

What type of incentives should you give your walkers?

I think it's important for the walkers to have incentives to work toward. It keeps them more involved and on their toes. I would *not* give incentives for time served. I used to give bonuses for time served and what I found was that it wasn't an incentive that improved the quality of the walkers. It simply improved the length they would stay and I don't necessarily want to give a poor walker an incentive to stay longer. The following are a few ways to give incentives to your walkers:

- *A bonus for referrals*: Give bonuses to walkers for referring new clients to you. You might even do a trial at offering a special bonus for the walker who refers the most clients to you.

- *Reward quality and productivity*: You can come up with certain standards of excellence you expect your walkers to achieve. For those who meet or even exceed that standard you can give a bonus.

- *Continuing education*: I would offer a bonus to walkers who agree to continuing education. For those walkers who agree to take safety classes at the Red Cross or want to learn a new dog training method with you, etc. you might give a bonus.

I would *not* give your bonuses in the form of an overall raise, continuing payment, etc. Instead I would give a *one time* payment to them.

The key areas of the relationship with your walkers are

- Screening.
- Hiring.
- Training.
- Monitoring.
- Firing.

Note: Training, Monitoring and Firing of walkers is discussed in detail in Chapter 11.

Screening Walkers

Hiring my first walker was nerve racking and the thought of being responsible for someone else's actions really scared me. I have since grown to be comfortable with the responsibility of overseeing thousands of weekly dog walks but it will likely take you some time to find a comfort level. Part of what has helped me is having systems, checks and balances that keep walkers productive and belief in the idea of hiring slowly and firing quickly.

If you can create a reliable pipeline of quality walkers coming into your company, you will have a huge edge on your competition. Doing so will also keep your training costs down and increase the loyalty of your clients.

Before you think about hiring, you need to decide what type of walker you want. In order to do that, think about the following questions:

- Who can you work with?
- Who matches your business philosophy?
- Who will your clients trust?

My intuition about hiring the right employees for my company has improved since I first started. It took me time to realize that the right employees for your company will not always be the smartest, most talented, or even the ones you like most.

The right walker for your company

I don't know you personally so I can't say what type of walkers would best suit your philosophy/needs. I can give you a list of some of the personality traits of my best walkers. They are:

- Easy-going.
- Reliable.
- Detail-oriented.
- Animal lovers.

- Good communicators.
- Interested in animal psychology / training.

Have I ever had a walker (including myself!) who embodies all of these traits? Probably not! But they are the things I look for in an applicant. And they are the words I use to describe our ideal walkers in prospective walker ads.

The following is a list of questions to think about for potential walkers and the careers they might be pursuing:

- *Actors:* What area of acting do they perform in? Theater? Television? Film? Do they rehearse at night? Do they have tryouts during the day that are short notice? Or can they schedule ahead around the job? Commercial and movie actors are definitely a flight risk if they work a lot. Actors are used to keeping schedules, receiving feedback and working in group environments, and that bodes well for dog walking.

- *Musicians:* Do they tour? How often and for how long?

- *Writers:* What type of writing do they do? Fiction or non-fiction? Abstract or analytical? For a newspaper or for themselves? The answers to questions like this will also point to their personality and behaviors. For example, I haven't found that abstract thinkers do well within a business structure.

- *Students:* I haven't had great luck with students. I feel their minds are usually elsewhere and you never know what their availability will be from one semester to the next.

- *Should I hire friends? Friends of friends? Friends of walkers? No!*

- *Should I do business with neighbors? People in my building? No!*

Remember: The best walker is not always the smartest, the nicest or the most experienced. The best walker is the one who is right for your company.

Where to find walkers

Craig's List (*www.craigslist.org/about/sites*) is a community site where you can post job listings for dog walkers. They cover most major cities in the United States and many smaller areas too. I have advertised in many other locations but nothing has compared to the success I've had on Craig's List. Job ads cost roughly $25 and I've advertised in both the ".etc" section and the "customer service" sections. You can find potential walkers on the street walking dogs but if Craig's List is big in your area, nothing will compare to the response you will get there.

What type of advertisement should you post?

Your ad should speak to your company philosophy, the demands of the job and expectations of the potential dog walkers. Your ads on Craig's List should also be eye catching with a nice image or logo included.

My recent Craig's List Job Advertisement went as follows:

> *Outdoors Type/Animal Lover wanted for part-time dog walking positions:*
>
> *Downtown Pets is a professional pet service in Lower Manhattan. We walk dogs individually, pay walkers per dog so there is an incentive to work and offer workers compensation and disability. Ideal candidates are reliable, detail oriented, outdoors types, dog lovers and are available Monday-Friday between the hours of 11am-4pm everyday. Please click the following link to learn more and to view our online application: www.downtownpet.com/ACCOUNT.html*

If you click the "NYC Dog Walker Application" in the link above it takes you to an information page on our website where you can also fill out a form. A web form is invaluable in helping filter potential applicants (information on how to create a web form are discussed in the Marketing Chapter).

If you would rather not do your own web form, you can create a survey at Zoomerang.com (*www.zoomerang.com*). The great thing about Zoomerang's Surveys is that you can export results into excel or Google Docs (discussed more in the Office Chapter).

Let's look at the questions on my web form (*www.downtownpet.com/ACCOUNT.html*), listed below. They will help you get an idea of what you need to know before even letting a walker get to an interview.

Where do you live?

A walker's proximity to your service area is obviously important. I would do everything possible to avoid walkers who live far away and/or need to rely on unreliable forms of transportation (subway line that's always shutting down, etc.). A walker not being able to make it into work due to transportation can lead to lost business.

Are you available Monday-Friday? And at the same hours Monday-Friday?

I personally need walkers who are available Monday through Friday and at the same time frames every day. Most clients will want consistency on the route, so a walker having a sporadic schedule is troublesome.

What are you applying for
(1. dog runner, 2. full-time dog walker, 3. part-time dog walker)?

Sometimes when I call a potential walker the answer over the phone is different from the answer they put down in their application. This is a small hint the person might not be reliable.

Best describe your intentions
(1. looking for quick way to make money, 2. do this while searching for another job, 3. can do this for at least 6 months, 4. can do this for at least 1 year)

I would stay away from those who answer one or two to this question. Why waste your time training someone if they could leave at a moment's notice? And lots of turnover will lose the trust of some of your clients.

Have you applied for any internships recently?

An applicant who has applied for an internship recently in a career they want to pursue could be a flight risk. Have they heard back yet? Even if they have been rejected this could be a problem because sometimes rejected applicants will later be accepted.

Most recent education? And highest education reached?

I'm not a college graduate myself but I've had the best outcome with walkers who were college graduates.

Are you pursuing a specific career? Which one?

I'd rather have a walker who is pursuing a career as opposed to one who is not. The benefit of a walker on a career path is they are unlikely to want to dog walk on their own. The negative is they might leave early for an opportunity they can't pass up. So it's your goal to find potential walkers who are pursuing a career but need a year or more to break into that career.

Do you have any vacations coming up? If so, when?

If someone has a three week family vacation to Italy already arranged they might not be a good fit.

Your experience with dogs is?

Some of my best walkers have had little to no experience with dogs. They have simply possessed great attention to detail and a willingness to learn and receive feedback. On the flip side many of my walkers who have owned dogs or been dog walkers before have brought bad habits with them. They look at things like hey I've walked dogs my whole life and never had a problem so why change now? This doesn't mean experience with dogs is a negative but don't shy away from hungry applicants who appear to be of good character just because they have limited experience.

As you see above you can rule out a potential applicant very quickly with the use of a web form or survey. Put the questions that are most important to you at the top of your form. When you look over the results if there's something you don't like you can immediately move to the next applicant, without having to read the entire form.

Researching your potential walkers on the web

You can discover much about an applicant just by searching their name or email address on the internet. You should be able to find personal websites, Facebook and My Space pages, and comments they have left on community pages. You might be able to learn much about your potential applicant based on the information you find.

Contacting potential walkers

Once you've narrowed down the walkers you want to contact make yourself a coffee or tea and set aside some time to call them. Take lots of notes while you speak to potential walkers. What should you look for in a phone call?

I start my conversation by asking if they are looking for part-time or full-time work. This should be a simple question but many of your applicants will fumble their answers, give you a different answer than they put in their application or ask you what you are looking for. This is your first sign of a bad applicant.

I then ask them if they are available Monday through Friday and at the same times everyday and listen closely to their answers. You might get: *"Uhh, well, I'm available full-time at the moment..."*

Your follow up should immediately investigate what "right now" means? Do they have a 2nd job? If so what are the hours? If they have a night job too you might have one exhausted walker during the day. Are they going to school? And if so are they only taking night classes? If not their class schedule might change next term and they will not be available.

At this point if the conversation is going well I usually try and establish a personal connection while at the same time learning more about this applicant.

Where are they from? How long have they been in the city? What career are they pursuing? What are some recent jobs they've had? Do they bad mouth some of their past employers? If so, that's a bad sign. The movies and music someone is into can sometimes speak to their thinking process too. This is also a time in the conversation to see if this person is engaged, lively, friendly and polite. Would you want to talk to this person on a daily basis? Would your clients?

If you don't feel good about this potential walker at this point you'll need to find a way out of the conversation. This is an area where I would not recommend saying what's on your mind. If you 100% don't see this person as a possibility in your company I'd find a polite way to say you'll see what happens.

You should be developing a sense of whether this applicant is an abstract thinker or not. If you're getting the sense they are an abstract thinker, someone really off the reservation, chances are they are not going to have strong attention to detail when it comes to your and your client's service requests.

All that's really left to find out are the financial requirements of your walker. I ask walkers what their monthly cost of living is, and I make sure the amount they need is realistic on the route they're applying for. It's important to know if this job is their only source of income, if they have money saved up, help from parents, etc.

Your first few conversations with a potential walker will provide you the information you need if you ask the right questions and listen closely. In those initial conversations you might learn more about some of your walkers than you ever will again. It's also your best opportunity to keep out potential troublemakers. I look for signs of a walker whose personal life is chaotic, who might be a bit careless, pushy, talk but doesn't listen, someone who has poor communication skills and or someone who might not be around long. A walker who is overly interested in how I run my business and the office side of the business could be a bad sign.

Meeting potential walkers

When I arrange to meet a new walker I make sure to give very specific details on where and when the walker should meet me (West 12th and Hudson on the southeast corner at 2:30 and please call my cell phone when you get there, etc.) This is your first test to see how detail oriented the potential walker is. Do they show up late? Early? Are they on the wrong corner? Do they stand there and wait for you or do they remember to call your cell phone? A walker making an error in meeting you is not a deal breaker, but it is something to make a mental note of. Watch and see if this is a trend.

When meeting a potential walker for the first time I like to go over some of the same questions we discussed on the phone and that they answered on the application. When are they available? What type of career are they pursuing? How might this effect their availability? Are their answers different than what they put on their form or said to you over the phone? Or has there been complete consistency in their answers? In the midst of sizing them up, try to create a connection on a personal level. Ask them their interests, where they are from, etc. and try and connect in some way.

Other things to look for when meeting a potential walker

- Do you enjoy talking to them? Could you see yourself talking to them on a daily basis?

- Are they presentable in how they are dressed?

- Do they look you in the eye when speaking or do they look down at the ground a lot?

- Try and pass by a dog or two while speaking with them and see how they react. Do they smile when seeing a dog and lean down to try and pet it? Do they not acknowledge it at all? Whether someone has experience with dogs or not, seeing a dog while they're with you should spark a positive reaction.

- Try and get a sense of if they will be around for awhile. Are they also applying for other jobs and if so are they entry jobs into their desired careers?

Let the potential walkers do the speaking. The more you let a potential walker speak the more chance you have to learn about their true intentions. This visit isn't meant for them to learn about the company, it's meant for you to size them up. If you're happy with them at the end of the talk then maybe discuss what it's like to be a walker with your company. If you're not happy with them, mention you're interviewing some more candidates and you'll see what happens.

A good way to keep the faith of your clients is to have low turnover with your walkers. That shouldn't stop you from firing bad walkers but it should motivate you to try and ensure you hire the very best walkers possible.

Some reasons for turnover

- A walker doesn't work out (gets fired).
- A walker leaves on short notice.
- There is not enough money on the route.
- Natural turnover based on time served.
- Client complaints.
- A walker is unhappy with the company.

Ways to avoid turnover

- Make sure the job can meet the financial needs of your walker.
- Incentive-based pay structure.
- Give raises over time.
- Test walkers during training.

Part-time vs. Full-time

There's a big difference between a full-time and a part-time walker for better and worse. Part-time walkers usually have a second job or are pursuing a career in the midst of working with you. The benefit of part-time workers is they usually require less income and can be less demanding. On the downside part-time walkers are often not available when you need extra help covering routes and you often can't grow their routes larger than they presently are. Part-time walkers are often less vested in my company than full-time walkers. A full-time walker probably sees the income from this job as his or her only form of income. The benefits of a full-time walker are they will likely want to work as much as possible so they can make as much as possible. A full-time walker will likely be available to help cover extra walks when you need it. On the downside a full- time walker might be more demanding in how much they need or want to make but this shouldn't be a problem if you can provide them enough work.

End of chapter checklist

- Hire a lawyer to consult with you on labor policies in your state.
- Create the strongest agreements possible that your lawyer says can be enforced in your state.
- Create a company handbook listing all of your policies.
- Decide how much you'll pay your walkers.
- Sign up for a payroll service.
- Choose the right time to add your first walker.
- Use a form or survey for your prospective walkers to fill out.
- Try to keep routes and dogs close to one another.
- Decide how much you should/can pay your employees.
- Decide who the right walker is for your company.
- Document your interactions and experiences with prospective walkers.

Chapter 11

Training and Testing Walkers

Training a walker

The moment has come to start training a potential walker and this will be the most important time you ever spend with your walkers. During the training period you could very well decide how good this walker will be. At the same time it's during training when you want to weed out bad applicants. There's nothing worse for you, or more expensive, than having a walker not work out. A bad walker can lose clients, create bad buzz for your company and just drive you mad. Do everything possible and beyond to screen potential walkers for reliability, trustworthiness, communication skills and the ability to receive constructive feedback.

I believe that you need at least 2 weeks to train and screen a new walker. The following is a breakdown of some of the things I do to train and screen my potential walkers.

Before a walker starts training

Before a walker starts training I'd highly recommend you consult your lawyer to see what type of form you can have the trainee sign. A trainee is not making you any money yet and you are spending a great deal of time training them; it is understandable if some states might not consider them employees yet. But again, you need to consult a lawyer on this issue because I can't say for sure how things work in your state. You can view our training agreement and other forms here:

Log on to *www.petsitterbible.com* > click the "pet service forms" tab

Note: I pay walkers for training but maybe you don't want to? Consult with your lawyer or accountant to see if you have to pay your walkers for training. At the very least maybe you can only pay your walkers for part of training. I think it's important to attract the best applicants, but I also know you will have many trainees who don't work out and that could cost you a lot of money. Try and find a system that works for both you and the walker. Maybe you could not pay a walker for training unless they complete a minimum of 5 days? But again you should consult a lawyer or accountant to make sure you can do this in your state.

Remember

You can only train your walkers once, so take advantage of this time. The time and effort you put into your training program will pay for itself ten times over if you do a good job. If you do a good job in finding the best walkers available and in training them well, you'll have a huge advantage over the competition.

10 Days of training

Day 1...

Few things provide a better way to bond than sitting down for a meal. I think it's nice to have your first day start with a coffee, bagel, whatever you like. During this time and every morning during training, try and get a better sense of them as a person. The more they find a friend in you the better chance you have to find out something they might have held back otherwise.

Before you get started have them fill out the following paperwork:

- *Personal information:* name, address, cell phone, cell phone carrier, emergency contact.

- *Training agreement:* This form will be based on what you and your lawyer come up with (independent contractor vs. employee, personal liability, etc.).

- *Must bring two forms of id and a utility bill.*

On the first day give them:

- A list of all your basic training guidelines.

- A list of your company philosophy.

Explain to them that every third day there will be a written test on what they have learned so far.

Set the tone from the first day that the more the walkers report back to you, the more money they can make. A professional dog walker has an impact on the dogs they walk. They notice when the dog is ill, injured or not house trained. Again, if all you do is run the dog out for a bathroom break, you could be replaced by the neighbor's kid. The walkers need to help you make your service invaluable to the clients.

On the first day I like to keep it simple when it comes to training. I usually cover the following:

- *How we walk dogs:* keeping the dogs in heel and on the left side of our body.

- *Pack Leader:* Explain how the walker needs to establish his or her role as pack leader and to walk through doors, across roads, into elevators, and past blind spots *ahead of the dogs.*

- *Danger areas:* In a city this might be stray voltage from lamppost. In a small town this might be traffic on a busy road.

- *No nos:* You can't listen to music, smoke a cigarette, drink coffee or constantly talk on the phone while walking a dog.

At first it was tough for me to let someone go at the end of the first day of training, but I've come to see the benefits in it. If someone is so obviously wrong for you and your company don't waste another moment with them. Save them and yourself time and you will also save yourself a lot of wasted money. If you're not sure what to say to someone in this situation, just tell them there was another person training you're going with. Or that an ex walker who used to work for you is coming back.

Make it clear from day one that the walkers work for you and not the clients. It is you who will have their backs when things are tough and you are in this together. The clients are not the enemy but the walkers are beholden to you, the company and not the clients' demands. The clients' demands are not always good for the company and sometimes they are downright dangerous for the dog. The walker must always involve you in decisions when they don't know the company policy already.

From the very beginning: Document concerns you have about the trainees. If they show up late, forget something, or irk you in anyway make sure you document it on paper, on your phone, etc. Memories are not always accurate. It's important to be able to present hard evidence to your walker or yourself when you have an issue with a walker.

Days 2 and 3...

On days two and three you want to reinforce training ideas from day one and further expand into basic dog psychology, including:

- The pack leader philosophy.
- Walking a dog in heel.
- Working with dogs who pull or stop.

- Teaching a dog to sit and stay.
- Meeting other dogs.
- Dogs who scavenge.

On day three I'd recommend giving your walker a written test on what they've learned up to this point. This test should give you a clear insight into how well the walker is picking up information.

At the end of day three you should also be getting a better sense for this potential walker. Have they been on time? Prepared? Involved? Engaged with you and the dogs? Are they concentrating on you when you speak or are their minds wandering? Do they have follow-up questions or just say yes to everything?

Have they lied to you or made excuse after excuse? Walkers who make up answers from the beginning are never going to be able to be trusted. Don't let a walker drain you slowly. If they show these character traits, get rid of them now.

Day 4...

Spend most of your morning session before walking dogs discussing puppies and house training in general (view training).

What if your dog gets in a fight with another dog?

A dog getting into a fight can be a very big deal. No matter who started the fight make sure to get the other dog owner's contact information. If your dog has been injured or cut in any way make sure to call your dog's owner immediately. Describe the situation to them and ask if they want you to take the dog to the vet. Even if you don't see any bite marks make sure to check the dog 10-15 minutes later. It can take 10 minutes for bite marks to even appear.

What if your dog attacks a person?

This is an even bigger deal than if your dog attacks another dog. Make sure you document the event in writing and contact the owner of the dog immediately. You never know when a situation might become a lawsuit. And you never know if your client will assume responsibility for their dog's actions. Often a client will not assume responsibility for their dog's actions and you will be forced to use your pet insurance. The first thing your pet insurance will ask for is a written account of the attack and phone numbers for any witnesses.

The walkers work for you, not the clients

If you and your lawyer have decided to classify the walkers as employees you need to make the walkers understand the chain of command. Your walkers work for you, not the clients! Clients will come and go but it's you two together for the long-term. It's not you and the walkers against the clients but when things get bad it's you and the walkers who will take care of each other.

Day 5...

Provide the potential walker a list of times they need to call you (forms). Give a test specific to house training (forms).

- Dog not home.
- Dog limping.
- Dog has blood in stool or urine.
- Diarrhea or throw-up.
- Dog barking (neighbor complaints).
- Dog going in the house/using wee-wee pads.
- Dog pulling on leash.
- If they are sick.
- Or unhappy.
- Or not making enough/ways to make more money .
- Start teaching them all the different equipment the dogs wear.

Start monitoring the walkers

It's ironic that many of the worst walkers I've ever had did great during training. This might be because I didn't test them with responsibility early enough in training. But this is a slippery slope because I refuse to allow walkers into clients' homes alone before we've have time to get to know them. As early as possible, and in as safe an environment as possible, I would test the walkers. Some ways to do that are:

- Leave money on a dining room table.
- Have dog's equipment not fit properly and have another walker waiting right outside the apartment check the equipment when they come out.
- Leave a "mess" out in an apartment.
- Have someone follow a "newbie" when he is walking alone.

Before letting walkers truly walk on their own, have them followed. Give them a few dogs to walk for a few days straight and have someone follow them (to check them out). Why? Because you need to see how they perform when they are alone in order to see their true colors.

Day 6...

- Continue teaching about equipment.
- Monitor the walkers.
- Discuss client interaction with them. Depending on how you and your lawyer have decided to classify the walkers will decide how much of their actions you control. If you've decided to make the walkers employees you can have the walkers not exchange phone numbers with the clients and direct all information to you. This is how I run my business. I have all scheduling, billing and training questions originate with the office to avoid confusion about what is

needed. I have also found this policy ensured the best quality of service. And it keeps my walkers operating within the structure of my company.

- Start getting the walkers used to being available on their cell phones while walking. Text them test reminders and see how well they do in replying to them. At this point the trainees need to start getting used to both walking dogs and receiving and processing information.

Day 7...

- Test on when they need to call you.
- House training.
- Continue teaching about equipment.
- Start testing them and let them walk a dog or two alone and monitor them.
- Continue getting the walkers used to being available on their cell phones while walking.

Day 8...

- Continue teaching about equipment.
- Continue testing them and let them walk a dog or two alone and monitor them.
- Continue getting the walkers used to being available on their cell phones while walking.
- Start training them on the route they will cover.

Day 9...

- Continue teaching about equipment.
- Continue testing them and let them walk a dog or two alone and monitor them.
- Continue training them on the route they will take over.

- Continue getting the walkers used to being available on their cell phones while walking.
- Teach the walker the basics of street PR, handing out cards and engaging dog owners to try and get their business.

Day 10 – The last day of training

- Continue teaching about equipment.
- Continue testing them, let them walk a dog or two alone and monitor them.
- Review the basics of street PR.
- Final written test.
- Continue training them on the route they will take over.

Personality

By this time you should be able to determine the following about your potential walker:

- If they are a dog lover.
- If they are organized and can keep a schedule.
- If they are trustworthy.
- If they have good communication skills.
- If they show attention to detail.
- If they are able to receive feedback.
- If they have learned how to use the equipment.
- If they will be around long.
- If they have a stable personal life.
- If they are walking the dogs as you've asked.

Beware: Be very careful with people who are extremely skeptical of you. You'll find some walkers want you to prove yourself to them and not just in the beginning but forever. Earlier in my company I used to try and please walkers like this but you never can. Certain people can never be pleased and still others will never trust you and you know the funny thing about these people? I've found that people who are usually endlessly skeptical of other *can't be trusted themselves!* Try and avoid these types of people if you can.]

Remember: Keep in mind how devastating a poor or incompetent walker can be for your business. Don't hire a walker just because they have finished your training period. If you don't trust them and if they have lost your faith, let them go and keep looking for a new walker.

Before you let a walker start working on his or her own

- *Have them sign your handbook:* Your handbook should detail everything covered in training and more.

- *Have them acknowledge your vacation policies:* At no time can more than one person be on vacation and vacations need to be short in our business. Try to have vacations start a day or two before a weekend or a day or two after a weekend (example: off Thursday, Friday, Saturday and Sunday). If more than one walker is on vacation this can cause serious problems with coverage and what if another walker got sick? Then you'd have three walkers out and that could cause major chaos.

- *Non-disclosure/non-compete:* If your lawyer says it's enforceable for you to have your walkers sign a non-compete and non-disclosure then definitely do it *before* they start working for you. You can view our example non-disclosure an non-compete forms in our forms chapter at the end of the book.

- *Give them a list of recommended items:* These items can range from great walking sneakers, to the best messaging cell phones to biodegradable waste bags. You can view our list in the forms chapter at the end of the book.

- *Require email/internet enabled phones:* It's essential that your employees be able to receive and send emails plus surf the web on their cell phones.

- *Get their W2/1099 information:* No matter how you and your lawyer decide to classify your walkers, make sure to get their W2 or 1099 information before they start working for you.

- *Give them updated dog notes:* Dog notes can be created in Google Docs and are the place you can update any changes to a dog's information (address, training issues, rules of the house, etc.). Ask your walkers to update their dog notes on a weekly basis or the notes will become old and unhelpful. You can view an example of our dog notes in the forms section at the end of the book.

- *Emergency contacts:* Your walkers should have emergency contacts for each animal they work with. They should have access to the clients' cell phone numbers, an emergency contact and the address and phone number of the dog's vet.

- *Key tags:* Make sure that all of your clients' keys are clearly tagged. When tagging a set of keys put the dog's name but no addresses in case you ever lose them.

Walkers and billing

Walkers play a very important role in the billing process. Make sure you have your walkers chart their numbers each day they work. Have your walkers chart their numbers on an excel sheet on their phone, through a web form, with pen and paper or on their computers. The point is to have your walkers document their routes in the moment. If you ask your walkers to chart their numbers at the end of a week or month they are likely to forget some jobs. If a job doesn't get invoiced then both you and the walker make no money!

End of chapter checklist

- Consult your lawyer to see what type of agreement a prospective walker can sign *before* training.

- During training give the prospective walkers a task where you can test them – ask them to meet you at different locations each day and at different times to see if they will follow directions.

- Keep detailed notes on how your trainee does.

- Does this trainee fit your personality?

- If you decide to hire the trainee make sure they acknowledge your policies, give them a copy of their route's dog notes and emergency contacts for the route.

Chapter 12

Engaging, Managing and Monitoring Walkers

Your new walker's first few weeks

The first few weeks with your new walker will be nerve racking for you and them. Keep in mind that the potential walker you found during training might not be the same walker you find once they are on their own. Why? People can just act different when not supervised. Here are some recommendations on how to manage your new walkers in the first few weeks:

- *Mornings*: I would meet your new walkers for a coffee or breakfast every morning for the first week or two. This is a nice way to discuss the issues you ran into on the past day and it's also a way to get to know the walker more.

- *The first three days*: During the first three days on their own I ask my walkers to text me after every walk. Their feedback should concentrate on issues they are experiencing, questions, feedback, etc.

- *Have them followed*: Have your new walkers followed a few days into the job. What do you see? Have they completely dropped doing everything you have taught them? Remember: *trust but verify!*

- *There will be mistakes*: New walkers will make mistakes, even mistakes that will make you scratch your head. I think it's important to expect that and you shouldn't immediately lose faith in your new walker. If you do lose faith in your new walker they will feel this and it will make things even worse. Expect mistakes to happen, address them when they do but also expect the same mistake not to keep happening.

- *See how new walkers take your feedback*: Things will move much faster once they get on a route alone. I like to start each day with a new walker by going over issues from the past day. See how the walkers take the feedback. Do they listen and accept it? Do they try and give you an answer for every issue you bring up? Do they seem to get annoyed and frustrated? Or do you seem like you might make them cry with the feedback? These are all important traits to take note of.

- *Take notes after your meetings with walkers*: It's important that you document the behavior of your walkers. You don't want to leave everything to your memory and gut feeling. Part of the decision or changes you'll need to make will be based on the walkers' factual history.

- *For first two weeks have each day mimic a day of training*: What I mean is take the theme for each day of training and apply it to a single day the walkers are alone on their route (example: one day on the route ask the walker to concentrate on putting the dogs in sit stays and then the next you can ask them to concentrate on checking the dogs).

Giving new walkers feedback

You should prepare your new walkers to receive lots of feedback in the first few weeks so they aren't surprised. Try to give your corrections with an even hand like:

> *"You're doing a great job, just do me a favor the next time this happens give me a call please before making a decision on your own. Sound good? Thanks!"*

How are you finding your new walker? Are they doing as well or even better than they did in training? Are they pulling a complete Jekyll and Hyde on you? Just as with a new client keep very close tabs on the performance of new walkers. Give them constructive feedback. Invite them to sit down with you for breakfast every few days during the first few weeks. If things are going badly try and address the situation in an optimistic, solution-oriented manner.

Lots of things can be worked on with a new walker except when it comes to safety. I would not let someone who is a safety risk work with my dogs for a moment longer, no matter the consequences for your business. A new walker who immediately ignores the safety guidelines in training is never going to work out.

Monitoring a walker

Once you've found a comfort level with your new walker it can be easy for you to stop talking and seeing each other very often. The whole point of having employees is to allow you to work on other areas of the business, right? But you must maintain a consistent level of contact with your walkers, both in person and through digital means too. This is a unique job in that your employees work for you but most of the time will be on their own, in a position to make decisions on their own. For an employer, not being in a position to supervise may be worrisome because you are responsible for your employees' actions.

The term I use in keeping walkers focused is to *nudge them* every once in awhile. There must be deadlines for your walkers to routinely meet. Maybe that means updating the notes on the dogs they walk? Maybe it means sitting down with you at least once a month to discuss their route, the job, etc.? Maybe that means surprising them on the route and walking with them for an hour, every so often?

Whatever avenue you take to keep your walkers focused, you need to stay on top of this. If you leave walkers to their own devices for an extended period of time, no matter how pleasant you find them on the phone, what you see with your eyes might surprise you. And that's a key point right there. Don't judge your walkers by how pleasant they are on the phone. Make sure to see it with your own eyes.

Document walkers

You need to document the experience with your walkers. Some items you might want to document:

- How many times a walker has been sick.
- How many times a walker has requested to be off.
- If a walker lies to you.
- If a walker is found to be cutting time on their walks.
- If a walker is difficult to deal with.

Mistakes will happen, of course, but look for clusters, trends and when they start to happen do your best to head them off with a correction, sit down, etc.

Communication / Passive Aggressive

A consistent trait of bad walkers I've known has been poor communication and/or passive aggressiveness. Some of the biggest successes have also been with walkers who had these traits but overcame them, partly through our interaction. Whatever the case, your walkers need to answer to you. If you treat them fairly and respectfully you have nothing to apologize for when it comes to that. Be wary of a potential or existing walker who has a hard time communicating important details. Very often if someone thinks they know what's best for them and the dogs and isn't very interested in ramifications, their actions could cost the company. You must be the one who is always looking out for the company's best interests and you can't always rely on walkers to tell you what they really think. Sometimes you need to decide for yourself what a walker's intentions are.

Keeping the walkers happy

I'll mention again that sitting down for a meal with an employee is a great chance to bond. If you happen to have things in common with the walker, it's obviously a gateway to a more personal connection. But even if you don't share mutual interests it helps to engage your walkers about the passions they are pursuing.

I've made it a habit to give my walkers presents over the years. Sometimes it's a small item like gel insoles for their sneakers or a gift card to Starbucks during the winter. Other times it's larger items like an EMS winter jacket or a cash bonus when a walker had a slow week. Walkers greatly appreciate these gestures and it makes me happy to know their days might be a little easier from the item I bought them. It also happens that these are tax deductible gifts, so it really is a win-win situation.

Important: Creating a human bond with your walkers is invaluable. If it's not instinctual for you make a point of doing so anyway. It's important that your employees know you are concerned about their welfare and happiness. If you are able to connect with your employees on a human level and they know it's authentic you will get more out of your employees. Why? You will have walkers who actually want to work for you and aren't just putting in their time and clocking out.

What makes a walker good?

The answer to this question will most likely reside in the type of company you want. Are you looking for walkers who are well versed in dog psychology and walk the dogs like champs? Or are you just looking for the dogs to have a best friend to play around with? A combination of both would be nice!

You might get lulled into thinking that a walker who shows up everyday and gets no complaints is a great walker. But again you need to see for yourself what is happening. A walker might be up for 20 dog walks a day but are they actually walking the dogs? Or are they just sitting on a stoop, talking on the phone? I personally would rather have a great dog walker here for 9 months who actually walks the dogs then a mediocre walker here for a year and a half who doesn't walk anywhere. The second walker could also be a financial liability when it comes to word of mouth about the company.

What makes a walker good in a client's eyes?

This is a tricky one because most clients will never actually see their walker with their dog. So a client bases their opinion of the walker on how they find their apartment when they come home, the notes the walker leaves and so on. You need to make it clear to the clients from the beginning that you actively monitor the walkers outside when they walk the dogs. A good walker in the home is not always a good walker out on the street. If you a fire a walker who was terrible outside with the dogs but great in the clients' apartments you'll need to make this distinction clear to the clients.

Google Docs/dog notes

Dog notes are collections of key information about your clients' pets, their homes, buildings, etc. I recommend you have your walkers update their dog notes on a weekly basis. I use Google Docs for our dog notes and I find them to be very helpful. I can invite a backup walker to a Google doc and they instantly have access to all the important information for the route they are covering. Imagine just a few of the issues a backup walker could experience walking a route that doesn't have updated dog notes. What if the dog is aggressive? What if the dog has allergies? What if the dog just got fixed and can't get wet or horse around? A backup walker can't walk a dog if they don't have updated dog notes.

Here's an example of one of Downtown Pets own Google Docs from a route: *www.petsitterbible.com/google_doc.shtml*

Backup walkers

One of the reasons clients come to a service is the benefit of a backup walker. If a client's regular walker needs to miss a day you need to have a backup plan. As I mentioned earlier one of the benefits to keeping routes in close proximity to one another is with backup coverage. Some keys to backup coverage are:

- *Updated dog notes*: You should have your walkers update their dogs notes (preferably stored in Google Docs) on a weekly basis. The dog notes information will include the dog's particulars like address, habits, behavior, rules of the house, if it's fed or not, etc. If a walker is out one day, especially on short notice, you will need updated dog notes.

- *Alert the clients*: Always alert clients when they will be a backup walker, before they have the backup walker. This is *very important* and not doing so is an easy way to lose the faith of your client.

- *All keys should be labeled*: Give all of your walkers a few extra key tags to carry around. All keys should be individually labeled.

- *Cut time if needed*: If you don't have enough able bodies to cover the normal routes then you'll need to cut time on the walks. Make sure to alert the clients you'll be doing this and assure them you'll charge them accurately.

- *Have backup walkers on call*: One idea is to have backup walkers who work from home but are always available if you need help. This isn't the ideal backup walker; I'd prefer to have someone who walks for me daily, but you might be able to make it work for you.

- *Ensure consistency with backups*: Do what is necessary to ensure the quality of service when your backups cover the walks. If things always go terribly wrong when a client has a backup walker they might not want backups in the future. And that would not be good for your company.

Very important: Clients must be notified *before* a backup walker shows up. A very easy way to lose the trust of your clients is to send over a walker they have never met, unannounced. Make sure to always inform your clients when they will have a backup walker and flood them with information.

Complaints about walkers

I was a walker myself, so I know what it's like to have complaints about me that are not true. Consider the source of the complaint and make sure you get the full story. An issue that requires your own investigation is if a walker is cutting time. People's sense of time can be distorted—did they actually look at their watch upon your walker entering the building and when they left or did it just "feel" short to them? A walker forgetting to do something requires a basic reminder. Safety issues require an immediate correction/meeting in person and possibly require you to fire the walker.

If one client complains about a walker cutting time, send out a group message to all walkers reminding them to stay tight on their times. If you have to engage the walker one-on-one, discuss the issue without mentioning the client. Remind the walker that they receive the same anonymity with complaints they may have about clients.

The manner in which you deal with problems (employees and clients) may determine your level of success and happiness. One of the greatest benefits in buffering the communication between walkers and clients is when it comes to dealing with complaints. You need to be the peacemaker and you also are there to provide an anonymous way for clients and walkers to voice complaints. If a client complains to me about a walker, I try to deal with the problem without mentioning the client. Sometimes, I'll send out a reminder to *all* the walkers to deal with just one issue.

When a walker makes a mistake

You can aim for perfection but it's only realistic to expect there to be mistakes. Mistakes in the pet service industry can be more pronounced than in most businesses! You are in someone's home alone with their dog, so if you were to forget to leave fresh water, to feed the dog or sign in, it can be a big deal for your clients. But is it a big enough deal that you should get upset or lose faith in your walker? Probably not! Unless this is a common theme with a walker, I would simply apologize to the client and give a reminder to the walker.

When *DO* you need perfection?

- When it comes to dogs in crates.
- Dogs with health problems.
- Dogs who are aggressive.
- Sleepovers and night walks.
- Telling the truth.
- Following safety guidelines (this is the biggest one for me).

Walkers will disappoint you. It's a sad truth but they, like you, are only human. What's important is *how* they respond to a mistake. Do they take responsibility and want to avoid making that same mistake again? Or are they passive and assume no responsibility?

If a walker does something to completely lose your trust, don't wait for them to disappoint you 2-3 more times before doing something about it. Get rid of a problem walker before they hurt your business even more.

Walkers who lie to you

Your walkers need to feel comfortable enough to tell you the truth. They need to know that you will forgive them for mistakes but you will not forgive them for lying to you. You need to part ways with a walker who repeatedly lies to you.

Working with people you don't like

I have definitely worked with walkers I didn't like personally, and it's hard to do. Sometimes the best potential walker will be a walker you don't like. But if they are a competent walker who loves dogs and is safety minded, sometimes you'll need to make allowances to grow your business.

As a walker ages

- A walker's performance will usually decline after the first 6-9 months.
- Try and find a way to keep them interested and involved: give them tasks and goals to meet.
- Over time a walker will physically break down: that's part of the reason it's in your interest to make sure the walker is using the best possible equipment and gear and that they take care of themselves.

What's better? A walker who has been here a long time but whose production has waned? Or a walker who is new, fresh, energized but you're not sure will work out? Is it better to chance improving your company vs. if it isn't broke don't fix it. You'll have to answer these questions for yourself once you decide your comfort level.

Walkers off-the-job issues

Some of the trickiest issues to control are your walkers' off-the-job issues. Some of these issues might involve:

- *Social life*: Some walkers like to hang out late and live hard. If you are aware your walker likes to drink a lot at night, has a problem waking up on time, etc. keep track of this. A walker who hangs out late at night can have less energy on the job daily.

- *Financial needs*: It's very important that you have a sense of the walkers' financial needs. Make sure you ask the potential walker to do a breakdown of their monthly expenses to ensure this job will yield enough money for your walkers to live comfortably.

- *When sick*: Does this walker take care of themselves when they get sick? Do they take the proper medicine? Do they get under the covers in bed and relax?

- *Friends and interests*: What type of friends and hobbies does this person have? Does this person surround themselves with healthy friends? Does this person live a normal social life? Or could you see their personal life affecting their performance on the job?

You can advise your walkers to try and live a healthy life but in the end it's really up to them. With that said though if a walker continues to make bad choices in their personal life you might need to consider firing them.

When to fire a walker

Being thoughtful, respectful and mindful of your employees' needs is essential in the modern workplace, but don't lose track of *your own* happiness. A win-win situation would be one in which your walker stays with you for 1-2 years, is happy, does a good job, is able to save up some money, and upon leaving the job, moves on to the profession of his dreams. But no matter how you treat your walkers there will be some, if not many, who don't work out. If you have a walker who is not working out I will assume you have documented their issues, as I mentioned doing earlier in the chapter.

Consider giving walkers a written warning that they have violated your policies and ask them to sign the form. If they refuse to sign it make sure you document that they refused to sign in it. If they happen to refuse to sign it things are probably not going to work out between the two of you anyway.

To fire a walker and not be responsible for their unemployment you will need to prove this walker's misconduct. The documentation of their misconduct can be done in writing, photo and or video. It will be helpful to have witnesses to the act who document and sign an account of what they saw (a walker consistently cutting time on walks; letting a dog off leash, etc.).

Remember: Before a walker joins your company you should have them sign your company handbook. Then you must document their breaking this agreement. With those two things you have a strong case in firing this walker.

When you are finally ready to fire a walker make sure you give them something in writing expressing that they have been fired. It has always been my way to sit down with a walker I'm firing and explain to them as little or as much as they want to hear as to my reasons. I then provide them the official letter they have been fired.

Think about: If the walker you are firing is friends with other walkers in your company you might need to do some damage control. I try and sit down with the friends of fired walkers to explain to them why I fired their friend and to make sure it's not causing a problem with them.

Think strongly about firing friends of the walker you just fired who are poor walkers/difficult to begin with. If I made one mistake in building my company it was not getting rid of disgruntled friends of walkers I had fired.

Important note: Every state has different policies on firing an employee so ask your lawyer or look into your state's policies before making a decision on firing a walker.

When a past walker goes after your clients

It's a sad truth but you will most likely experience a past walker trying to steal clients from you. Some walkers will not want to move on from dog walking and some clients will build a personal connection to their walkers. But if you take a few basic steps to protect yourself, employees stealing clients shouldn't keep you up at night. I've encountered the issue of ex clients working with ex walkers in *less than 1%* of the clients who have ever been at Downtown Pets. And this is a liberal estimate! The number really might be less than .5% of all clients who have ever been clients at Downtown Pets. I'm factoring in that there have been a few more instances I'm not aware of but even then the overall amount is miniscule. And yet until recently it has driven me a little crazy when it's happened because I've taken it personally. I've dedicated way too much time to this issue and I want to help you handle this issue better than I did at first. Don't get me wrong; it's important to defend your company but you also need to look at things in percentages as discussed before and see the big picture.

If you're keeping track of your business and "nudging the walkers" as I mentioned earlier, theft of clients shouldn't be too much of a problem. I also feel that career minded walkers will pose less of a concern. If you made sure to have your walkers sign agreements before starting you have a strong legal case to make them stop. Walkers who respect you will most likely back off, especially if you remind them of the agreement they signed with you too (assuming you did draft an agreement with your lawyer). There will always be the rare few who don't get why it's a problem nor understand nor respect everything you tried to provide them. Whatever the case I'd try and engage the walker through email a few times and remind them of their signed agreement. If they completely ignore these reminders, I'd ask your lawyer to provide a cease and desist letter.

Remember: Don't fall in love with your clients or your walkers! And try to look at things in percentages. Try and remove emotion from the equation as best you can. Being prepared psychologically ahead of time should lessen the blow if it happens to you.

Best ways to avoid it

- *Having a lawyer draft a strong agreement*: As you've noticed I can't stress enough how important it is to involve a lawyer (who specializes in your state's labor law) before hiring someone. But even if you already have existing walkers you should still hire a lawyer to write up the strongest agreement possible. A strong legal agreement will scare most walkers off even the idea of stealing clients from you afterward. But if a walker violates your agreement you also have the peace of mind that you could pursue an action against them if necessary. You are not guaranteed a victory by having a legal agreement but your position is greatly increased. Plus the fear of a lawsuit alone will scare some troublemakers off.

- *Communication goes through the office*: If you enforce the policy of not having clients communicate directly with walkers (through phone or email) then it should help keep clients' allegiance to you.

- *Help the clients with their problems*: Continuing to educate yourself on dog training solutions will keep the goodwill of your clients. If you are able to help the clients with the issues they are having with their dogs, this will make you and your service invaluable to the clients.

- *Stay engaged with the clients*: Respond to clients' emails and phone calls in a speedy fashion. Show them the benefits of dealing directly with you.

- *Have the clients understand what you do for them*: Some clients have no clue what you, the owner, do for them on a daily basis. Add a page on your website, a link on the page dedicated to clients' issues, to talk about some of the things you personally (in the office) provide for your clients.

The unexpected benefits of walkers being disloyal

I'm not recommending that you leave yourself exposed to having to experience disloyalty from someone. But if you do happen to experience disloyalty you might learn a lot from the experience. It might make you think about the type of walkers you've been hiring. Are they right for your company? I have learned a lot from bad and disloyal walkers actually. I have learned who the right walkers for my company are (both for me personally and my clients). I have also discovered that certain walkers are right for certain routes, areas, etc. based on their personalities. I discovered the following by having one bad apple in an area surrounded by *many* other walkers:

What I learned is that if you're going to have a cluster of routes in a busy dog walking area you need to carefully choose the walkers for those areas. Most successful in areas of this type have been walkers who are pursuing a career outside of the job, are more into walking dogs well than socializing and are actively engaged with me.

Should you sue a past walker who has stolen a client

How many clients has this past walker stolen? Can you afford the costs of suing them? Sometimes reminding a past walker of the financial ramifications of breaking their signed agreement is enough to make them stop (discuss creating a signed agreement and involving a lawyer). I would only sue a walker if it is beneficial to your business. Is this walker friends with lots of other walkers? Could they create a cancer in your company? If so and you can afford to maybe you should investigate suing them. But I would choose to go one direction or another. And no matter the answers to these questions *I'd involve your lawyer* to advise you. If you decide not to sue them don't waste too much time letting the issue bother you. Spend your time and energy trying to improve your company and maybe take some steps to avoid this happening again. A client who would work with one of your walkers on the side is usually a bad client to begin with. Be happy to be done with both the walker and the client, no matter what you decide to do.

Never stop looking for good walkers

In baseball they say you can never have too many good pitchers and in our business you can never have too many good walkers. When your company seems the most secure in regard to employees, it is the best time to work hardest to make sure you have potential walkers in case something were to go wrong. I try and spend at least 30 minutes a day, *every day*, going through new walker applications and making phone calls.

Keep your existing walkers engaged and interested

Give walkers incentives and projects to keep them interested in their jobs. What I've tried to do is take the strengths of a walker and apply it to their present job.

If you have a walker who is a good writer maybe they can help you write a script for a promotional video? If you have a walker who is a great speaker maybe you can have them be your PR point man. This would be the person you sent to vet

offices to spread the word about your company. You might have another walker who is great with office work. Maybe they can help you in the office during slow days? Maybe they can even become your assistant over time? The point is to try and engage your good walkers and keep their interest in the job. Being able to combine a walker's interests from outside the job onto the route can be very beneficial to you and the walkers.

Another idea: Take your best walkers who seem to love your company and perform the job best and raise their status. Train a walker to help you train new walkers. Doing so will allow you to spend more of your time expanding the company.

Protecting yourself against walkers leaving on short notice

A walker leaving on short notice can be devastating to your business and your life. If a walker doesn't give you enough time to prepare a new walker for the route you could very well lose that route. Or if not you will be forced to run around like crazy covering an extra route. Here is some advice to protect you against walkers leaving you early:

- *Company handbook*: Include something in your company handbook about giving at least 3-4 weeks notice before leaving.

- *Incentives for notice*: Maybe give some financial incentives for the walkers to give notice before leaving.

- *Always look for new walkers*: It doesn't matter if you are chock full of walkers. You need to make sure you are always talking to potential walkers. You never know when you might need a new walker whether it be for expanding your company or covering a walker who is leaving on short notice.

- *Beat them to the punch*: If you know a walker is not going to stay with you long then you might want to fire them at your convenience. If someone has told you that a particular walker has been talking about leaving soon, but that walker hasn't told you, then prepare as if they are leaving within the month.

Reasons walkers can become disgruntled

- *Money*: Know how much a walker needs to make *before* they start working for you. If a walker's financial needs increase while working for you or if what they're making decreases you need to address this. Try not to hire walkers who have exceptionally high financial needs compared to what you can pay them.

- *Workload*: You should also know how much a walker can/wants to work *before* they start working for you. If you need a walker to work longer hours or cover more distance than you originally promised them you need to discuss this with the walker. Make sure you don't push your walkers past their breaking point. If you do you will likely lose walkers with short notice.

- *Feeling disrespected*: Many dog walkers can be sensitive when it comes to feedback and I think it's for two reasons. One they are spending most of their days working on their own and they are not used to getting that much feedback while performing their job. Secondly, most walkers are pursuing a career outside of the pet service industry. Your dog walkers might love working for you and walking dogs but they also might be sensitive when it comes to feedback. Make sure you deliver your feedback with respect, and I'd recommend that you always give some praise first. Like you are doing a great job with this but I'd like you to work on this. It's also important that you periodically give your walkers feedback. If you never give your walkers feedback and then pour it on them all in one shot it might be hard for them to receive.

End of chapter checklist

- Stay engaged with your walkers once they are on their own.
- Trust but verify – make sure you see your walkers performing their jobs without them always knowing they're being monitored.
- Give the walker feedback to see how he or she takes it.
- Show your walkers respect and support.
- Walkers will make mistakes but hopefully not more than once.
- Walkers must be perfect when it comes to safety.
- A walker who isn't interested / concerned with safety issues might not be right for your company.
- Your walker's off-the-job issues can be as important as their on-the-job issues.
- Unless your walker has lost your faith, defend them when it comes to client complaints but make sure the issues are addressed.
- Take steps to avoid losing clients to past walkers (chief among them being a non-compete if allowed and enforceable in your State).
- Never stop looking for good walkers, even when you don't need any.
- Get rid of problem walkers.
- Stay engaged with the owners to limit fallout when you fire a walker.
- Come up with policies and incentives to protect yourself against walkers leaving.

Chapter 13

Going Forward and Final Thoughts

Going Forward

I hope you have found this book to be as helpful to you as it's been for me! I've learned so much myself in writing this book and it's helped my own company. I've been able to study the things I've been doing right but more importantly the things I can improve. Not everything I've written in this book represents my own policies but they represent the best I could hope for in my business. I've learned so much in writing this book that I have a whole new list of goals and objectives to shoot for now.

Be like a whale

A whale never stops moving, even when it's sleeping! And that's what your company needs to be like. You always need to keep moving and adapting to the changing business landscape. Some areas you should continue to improve over time:

- *Website look and promotional materials*: I look at some of my competitor's websites and it looks like they were made in the early 1990s. You need to make sure your website stays fresh and over time I'd highly recommend doing a redesign of your website. When you do a redesign of your site you can take the new look, logo, etc. and apply it to new business cards, post cards and stationery.

- *Website/technology upgrades*: On top of the design of your site over time you should upgrade the features of your website and your office. *Example*: I recently added a comments feature to my vet and pet store listings. But you also want to make sure you stay on top of improvements in cell phones, computers, email, calendar or accounting software.

- *New services*: You should add or improve the services you offer over time. *Example*: We recently started to offer guaranteed coverage on Saturdays and that has worked. In another example we started to offer sick day services when our clients were home sick. We offered the service of bringing them drinks, medicine, magazines, etc. for a small fee. But this service hasn't garnered any interest so we have since stopped offering it. The point is that you should try out new things and improve things that already work over time.

- *Stay on top of the trends*: Is there amazing new equipment out there for dogs? Is there new accounting software on the market that could save you 3-5 hours a week of work? Has it become easy to add dynamic features to your website that years ago would have been impossible? Is it possible now to create a mobile app for your clients' cell phones? Stay on top of the changing trends in your industry and in technology.

- *Continue to educate yourself*: You can never know enough about the pets you service. Here are some recommended resources about pets and the pet service industry:
  1. Modern Dog Magazine

2. Dog Fancy Magazine
3. *www.dogster.com* (Website)
4. "It's Me or the Dog" (Television Show - Animal Planet)
5. "Pitbulls and Parolees" (Television Show - Animal Planet)
6. "Dogs 101" (Television Show - Animal Planet).

- *Business Resources*: Here are some recommended *business* magazines, books and t.v. shows you might find helpful:
  1. Inc. Magazine
  2. Entrepreneur Magazine
  3. Mac World Magazine
  4. PC World Magazine
  5. Website Magazine
  6. Built to Last (the book)
  7. Success Built to Last (the book)
  8. Pour your Heart into It (history of how Starbucks was built)
  9. Your Business (TV show on MSNBC).

- *The dogs and the walkers*: There's nothing more important than the safety of your dogs and the happiness of your walkers. Take care of both and you should have a successful company.

- *One thing at a time*: I think we can all be victim to not seeing things all the way through and I sure used to have that problem. I have grown to adopt a philosophy that has helped me with this and it's to do one thing at a time. Sounds simple right? Try it out and see something all the way through and then go from there.

- *Be productive not busy*: Some of us feel guilty if we're not manically busy. Try and be more productive than busy.

- *Let the small things go*: I used to routinely get angry about way too many small things. I was famous for smashing my cell phones to pieces, that's how bad my anger problem was. I have since though started to try and see the big picture. Now I try and let the small things go and I'm much happier for it. How have I been doing it? I realized that it would be hard at first. I realized that the first few times I'd get angry it would be close to impossible not to explode. But I also realized that if I could get through those first few times it would get easier and easier and it has!

- *Inject your personality into your company*: Are you funny? Artistic? Concerned about animal welfare? Find a way to inject your personal beliefs into some area of your business. For me that involved taking my company green and doing this makes my days just a little bit more enjoyable. You can learn more about how I took Downtown Pets green here: *www.downtownpet.com/green_dog_walkers_clients.html*.

- *Raise prices*: As I've mentioned earlier you need to raise prices over time. The easiest way to create increased cash flow in your company is to raise your prices. If you're doing a good job with your business and have earned your clients' trust, you shouldn't lose many clients at all from a rate increase.

- *Improve your process for finding, training, managing walkers*: Your ability to create a steady pipeline of great walkers coming into your company will help separate you from your competitors. Learn from the problems you experience with your walkers. See every new walker as an opportunity to get things right with problems you experience with your walkers.

- *Raise the status of walkers*: Hire from within your company. Raise the status of some of the walkers you most trust to help train new walkers. This will lessen your work load, make the job more appealing for those walkers and also help you keep tabs on what's going on in your company.

- *Train an assistant*: Over time you should hire at least a part-time office assistant to free you up more as your company grows.

- *Train someone to back you up*: Whether you hire an assistant or not make sure to have someone in place to cover your responsibilities if you were to get sick or go on vacation.

- *Take vacations*: You need to take time off! Do what is necessary, starting with preparing backup coverage for yourself and make sure to decompress periodically.

- *Stay ahead of the competition*: Some pet services remain 3-5 years behind the trends. Their websites are not actively updated and their resources are ancient. Make sure you are not too far ahead of the trends or too far behind. Stay on top of how your industry is changing and I'm confident you'll know the right time to make changes to your company.

Gossip and Buzz

Over time your company will start to create buzz in the areas you work. Hopefully, it's good buzz that you are creating because dog owners talk to other dog owners out on their walks. There's no better marketing tool for your company than a happy customer recommending your services to prospective clients. On the flip side there's nothing worse for your company than a disgruntled ex-client or employee bad mouthing your company. The problem with so many people discussing your company is the facts will start to get mangled. Do you know the game telephone? You line up five children and whisper a word into the first child's ear and then they whisper the word into the child next to them and so on. When you ask the last child in the row what the word is it's usually much different than the word you told the first child. This is what gossip is like and why it's so dangerous.

I don't like to gossip and I hate when others gossip about my company, especially when they are factually wrong. Make no mistake people will gossip about you and your company but hopefully it will be positive things. If it's not and your company starts to get bad buzz you should take steps to combat this bad buzz. You might do this by getting the word out to your walkers and friends in the area what the truth is. Or you might make changes to your company to combat the bad buzz.

The following is a quote from the movie *"Doubt"* and for me it perfectly shows the danger of gossip. (A priest talking to a woman about how she's been gossiping about others)

> *"I want you to go home, take a pillow up on your roof, cut it open with a knife, and return here to me!"*

So the woman went home, took a pillow off her bed, a knife from the drawer, went up the fire escape to the roof, and stabbed the pillow. Then she went back to the old parish priest as instructed.

> *"Did you gut the pillow with the knife?"*
> *"Yes, Father."*
> *"And what was the result?" "Feathers," she said.*
> *"Feathers?" he repeated.*
> *"Feathers everywhere, Father!"*
> *"Now I want you to go back and gather up every last feather that flew out on the wind!"*
> *"Well," she said, "it can't be done. I don't know where they went. The wind took them all over."*
> *"And that," said Father O'Rourke, "is gossip!"*

- FROM THE MOVIE "DOUBT"

Can you get too big?

Yes! There is a business philosophy that says one person *can't effectively manage* more than 150 people at a time. I can definitely affirm this philosophy. I never got over 150 but I did get close, once getting up to 147 people! Honestly my business was a little chaotic at that size with just me managing it. Make sure you hire someone to help you out in the office and/or in the field as your company grows. Never sacrifice quality for profit. Having your company get too big too fast, without organization, is a prime way to lose control over the quality of your company.

The discussion doesn't stop here!

Come and join us at our website (*www.petsitterbible.com*) and also through our social pages (visit *www.petsitterbible.com/mobile*). There you will find fellow pet service professionals discussing the day-to-day lives of their businesses. On our website you will also find:

- *Product links*: We will post links to many of the products we have mentioned in this book. You'll be able to learn more about them and purchase them if you like.

- *Discussion board:* On our discussion board you can raise and answer questions relating to the pet service industry. Come be a part of the discussion!

- *Image and video tutorials:* On our website you will find lots of helpful image and video tutorials.

- *View updates to this and future books:* We will post updates to this and future books published by Downtown Pets.

Hope to see you there!

To close I hope you have found this book helpful and I hope you come back to it and our website when you run into problems in the future. I'll leave you with some of the keys that have been instrumental in Downtown Pets' success:

- I've always kept our animals safety and happiness as my primary concern.

- I've treated my walkers with respect and tried to pay them fairly.

- I've spent more time trying to find good employees than getting new clients. My belief has been that by providing excellent employees the clients will come and they have.

- I have put a huge emphasis on my websites and my placement on search engines.

- I've always told my clients the truth and have demanded the same from my employees.

- I've tried to provide exceptional customer service.

I'd like to end with a few quotes that have had a profound impact on my life

"You can't control how you feel but you can control what you do."

— DON KAPLAN

"If you want to work for the New York Times start by sweeping their floors."

— DON KAPLAN

"Just do it."

- NIKE

"No one gives it to you. You have to take it."

— JACK NICHOLSON IN "THE DEPARTED"

And Finally...

I wish you well and I hope you're excited. You're about to embark on the coolest career imaginable.

You're going to work with animals for a *living*!

www.petsitterbible.com

www.downtownpets.com

www.nycdogrunners.com

Made in the USA
Lexington, KY
29 December 2011